Guiding Adults

Guiding Adults

James D. Williams

Convention Press / Nashville, Tennessee

5161-10
This book is number 6110, area 1,
of the Christian Leadership Courses
of the New Church Study Course
Library of Congress catalog card number: 78-91972
Printed in the United States of America
15. s 69 R.R.D.

Contents

Contents, continued

Preface

WRITING A BOOK of this nature has been an immensely challenging and rewarding experience. To bring together insights from the related fields that comprise Christian adult education is no easy assignment.

In every sense of the word this is a "transition book." It is called an intraprogram book. It is written to adult leaders of all the church program organizations. The former "teaching" books in the Church Study Course series were written for a particular program organization.

This is a transition book because it reflects changes that are taking place in the educational world. Many of these changes can be seen in very embryonic forms within present programs of Christian adult education. New techniques of instruction, within easy grasp of any church, could revolutionize the Christian teaching and training of adult learners.

The earnest desire of the author is that the reader, after having studied the book, will develop a better understanding of the learning leader's role and the logic which he must master. Leading adults in learning can be an exciting adventure or it can be a frustrating, disillusioning experience. The more skilful you become in the performance of your role the more rewarding and meaningful will be your role.

The Christian education of adults is imperative in the critical times in which we live. The investment of your life in this worthy endeavor will be a significant contribution in God's redemptive work in the world.

A special debt of gratitude is expressed to those who have made it possible for me to prepare this volume. Particularly am I indebted to my colleagues at Southwestern Baptist Theological Seminary, some of whom have been my teachers. Many of the concepts in this book were first developed in their classes. I would voice special thanks to the late Lee H. McCoy who introduced me to the field of adult education.

In my years of teaching, I have learned most from my pupils. The exciting and stimulating experiences of the classroom have been a constant source of personal reward. To all of you who have shared in these experiences, I voice grateful thanks. Especially would I single out those doctoral students whose research efforts have been of special value to the preparation of this manuscript. Wayne Summers is due special recognition for the work he did in connection with chapter three.

Finally, I wish to express deepest gratitude to my own family for the patient way they endured the demands of a project like this. Above all I must give credit to my wife, Jo Williams, who was a faithful typist and critic, helping me keep my feet to the ground. Any strengths of this book are to be credited to my parents, teachers, students, and family. Any weaknesses are mine.

JAMES D. WILLIAMS

Fort Worth, Texas
July, 1969

Guiding Adults

1

Learning
in the Christian
Community

IN A DAY when great stress is being placed upon adult education in the social, political, economic, industrial, and every other area of life, a special responsibility is laid upon the church to become a teacher.

The whole world has become a classroom! Through magazines, newspapers, television, and radio, learners of every age are appropriating truths, half-truths, and "no truths." Out of this maze of learning is coming knowledge which is both enriching and damaging life.

The accessibility to learning is putting many people into contact with experiences and areas of life that previously had been reserved for comparatively few. If we, in our society, are to avoid developing one-sided or fragmentary personalities, the Christian community must do its part.

Adults in our world desperately need to be led into new areas of religious life and experience, as well as new areas of religious knowledge. Many leaders in adult education in the church fear that a widening chasm has developed between Christian and secular adult education. Is it necessary for this chasm to exist? Perhaps we should remember that education is incomplete when it only equips the adult with knowledge and skill in making a *better living*. There must also be that education which provides the learner with knowledge and skill for *living better*.

How shall we live better? In a broad sense, this concerns our problems of living and working together, intelligently and in goodwill, while we strive to build a more worthy society. This is the problem of *human relations*. In an individual sense, it concerns the person himself. It concerns his inner equipment of attitudes and motives, for it deals with the things he wishes to do and to be. This is the problem of *personal growth*.

This problem of personal growth, of building a better life, is essentially a problem of the Christian religion. It is out of a person's concept of Christian principles and values that he determines what the better life is—for himself and for the society in which he lives.

The task of adult education in the church is to bring the adult into a dynamic encounter that provides an interpretation of the Christian life. He must be led to enter it through faith in Christ, and then be guided in the continued living of it.

Continuous Learning for Maturing Minds

"But when I became a man, I put away childish things" (1 Cor. 13:11). For the average person, this process is not as easy as it sounds. Not every adult is mature; moreover, every adult is immature in some respects. Even though a person has "grown up" in the sense of becoming an adult, he is not yet finished with physical, mental, and physiological changes.

The New Testament teaches that man is not "grown up," but is in the process of "growing up." The apostle Paul expressed this idea in a rather penetrating manner when he wrote, "I count not myself to have apprehended: . . . I press toward the mark" (Phil. 3:13-14).

It is clearly evident that the Scriptures admonish us to continue in learning. Can you think of some other reasons for doing so? Consider these reasons.

1. *A changing world makes it necessary to continue to learn.*
—As the world becomes smaller with jet travel, space exploration, and mass communication, some adults feel overwhelmed and tend to withdraw. Such an isolationist stance may cause these adults to become narrow-minded and prejudiced. Restrictions breed fear, and fear conquers the world-mindedness and concern that Jesus wanted us to develop. This kind of fear also tends to accent man's sense of smallness in a complex and highly technical world.

Yet this is precisely the kind of world in which personality and life are developing. The changing nature of our world requires that adults maintain a vigorous idealism. At the same time, they need practical ability for dealing with the realities of life. The Christian adult believes that the needed power is available through Jesus Christ, who said, "I am come that they might have life, and that they might have it more abundantly" (John 10:10).

Change is inherent in human nature. We cannot escape change. Although a person may carry the same name throughout life, he is not always the same person—physically, psychologically, socially, mentally, or spiritually. He is a changing person. Are your needs, interests, attitudes, abilities, and ideals the same as they were ten years ago? Obviously not! The changes which have taken place in you have caused you to rearrange your mode of living, to alter views, and to adjust to new relationships.

Change and growth cannot be separated from life, because they are characteristic of life. An individual has only to look at an old photograph of himself or to read from a diary of school days to see obvious evidences of change. A person can neither deny nor escape the outcomes of change inherent in human nature and personality.

Not only can you observe the changes which continue to take place within you, but you can also see those changes beyond you. There are national and international changes. In our nation, the economic and social structure is changing. Labor is developing into a powerful political force. Racial intolerance is cutting at the foundations of democracy. A growing conflict between nationalism and international cooperation is emerging. It is unlikely that you will relate yourself to the changing world if you are content to remain where you are in established patterns of thought and action.

The very nature of learning demands change. Perhaps it is now time for us to consider a definition of learning. In most definitions of learning, there are some common words like "change," "behavior," "practice," or "training." Learning could be variously defined. Perhaps an acceptable definition is *a change or origination of behavior resulting from experience.*

Unfortunately, the psychologists of the nineteenth century labored under the false notion that adults were incapable of learning. They believed that outside his own business, an adult could learn nothing after he reached age twenty-five or so.

This mistaken notion was seriously challenged when the adult education movement began to flourish during the early part of this century. After very careful and extensive scientific investigation, psychologists discovered that learning can continue throughout life.

Though there may occur some measurable decline in *speed* or *rate* of learning ability in advancing years, this decline is due primarily to lack of practice. Continual use of a person's mental abilities causes them to be of greater value throughout life.

Adults can find assurance in the fact that there are certain faculties of the mind that tend to improve with age. Can you identify some of these? Did you think of faculties such as vocabulary, judgment, reason, rote memory, and creative imagination?

Having recognized that learning is possible as long as life lasts, adults by the millions are involved in all types of learning experiences. These experiences cause adults to differ from their former selves.

In summary, we may conclude that Christian living is characterized by change. Christian educators believe that a person cannot progress so far down any path of thinking or action that he cannot be transformed by the power of God.

Christian conversion is a definite change. The apostle Paul referred to it as a change to a "new life" (2 Cor. 5:17). The search for this new life is a creative act of the mind involving change in the person who learns.

After conversion takes place, the Holy Spirit continues to bring change. The believer is instructed in righteousness, convicted of sin, and led to faith and action.

A redeemed adult sincerely desires to become like Christ. When a believing adult submits himself to the lordship of Christ, the changes which occur in his thoughts and actions are miraculous.

2. *The power of influence makes it necessary for adults to continue in learning.*—No adult is without authority and influence over someone. He may be parent, teacher, officer, foreman, or simply a member of a majority group. Many adults exploit and selfishly use their influence for personal gain. Can you recall some people from the pages of history whose powers of influence were adult, but whose motives were infantile? The adult has certain powers that are denied the infant and youth. Therefore, the improper exercise of influence can be a most dangerous and harmful thing.

Adults have a great amount of influence over children and young people. Children and youth tend to become like those with whom they live. The influence of adults upon their lives is far more significant than the standards and ideals taught by the church and school.

The apostle Paul lived such a maturing life that he could honestly admonish those under his influence to imitate him. Do you want others to become like you? The challenge of such a thought should prompt you to continued study and growth in order that your life may be improved.

3. *Obedience to Christ makes it necessary that adults con-*

tinue to learn.—Our Lord makes it very clear that all men should be lifelong disciples or learners. Jesus himself grew mentally, physically, spiritually, and socially (Luke 2:52).

What will happen if adults go on learning in every other area of life and experience but stand still religiously? An imbalance of growth can cause serious damage to faith and resultant action.

Adults need to be "thoroughly furnished unto all good works" (2 Tim. 3:17) and to "grow in grace" because our Lord commands it.

CHRISTIAN LEARNING AS TRANSFIGURATION

Learning involves a transformation of the heart as well as of the mind. Our very capacity for learning is a reminder to us of the integrative nature of all personal knowledge. We are changed or reshaped by what we know.

Charles Stinnette reinforces this fact when he states:

> Learning is an integrated and integrating act. It involves the personal organization of experience and results in the transformation of a problematic situation into an ordered one. The achievement of order is perceived as a result of both personal and public agency. It does not occur in a vacuum. In knowing, the human being is exercising his responsible selfhood. He is both participating in a community of given meanings, and, at the same time, creating new meanings which shape the future of that community with the imprint of his own personality.[1]

Learning and what you are as a person are inseparable. Values of life are learned in the same stadium of choice where we discover the ways to gain desired goals. The question is, To whom and to what have you given yourself?

Paul reminded the Roman Christians of their new life and identity in Christ. They were to resist passive adaptation to the pattern of the world, and open themselves to the change and transformation that could come through the Spirit of God.

The Christian, therefore, must choose to be changed. God insists that man choose. He does this by confronting man with the various idols he serves. Jesus' statement, "Ye cannot serve God and mammon" (Matt. 6:24), suggests that man must decide for or against God.

In a sense, Christian adult education must begin with the question, Who is Lord? The sovereignty of God is the first lesson we must learn. One adult said to a Christian helper, "It's my life; I'll do with it what I want." The question remains, Who is the creator of life? It is obvious that this person had chosen to ignore the sovereignty of God.

Repentance becomes the heart of transfiguration. The imperative *to change* means a decision to turn from one way of living to another. If there is a difference between secular and Christian adult education, it is here.

The learner's accessibility to Christ as a transforming power is mediated by the Spirit. The Christian community living in covenant is rooted in repentance and called into existence by the Spirit.

What, then, is the relationship of the Christian community to adult learning? There is more to this question than can be answered in a few pages, but basically there are two pointed aspects of this relationship.

First of all, the adult learner enters into the community by way of repentance, through his own consent. An amazing concept of the Bible is that God's freedom includes the corollary of man's freedom. Secondly, repentance represents the learner's response to God's prior grace. Repentance cannot be learned. It, like transformation, is made possible by the Spirit. As the living Word of God is addressed to the individual through the covenant community by the Spirit, the learner is set upon his feet through repentance and readied for ministry. Such a divine, dynamic, and changing force is a special ingredient that the secular adult learning experience can know nothing about.

In summary, learning as transfiguration is a reality when man, upon being summoned to dialogue with God, responds in repentance and faith. Such a divinely initiated resource made available to man becomes the highest and greatest source of growth that man can obtain.

The words of the apostle Paul provide a fitting summary to this idea. He said, "Therefore, my brothers, I implore you by God's mercy to offer your very selves to him: a living sacrifice, dedicated and fit for his acceptance, the worship offered by mind and heart. Adapt yourselves no longer to the pattern of this present world, but let your minds be remade and your whole nature thus transformed" (Rom. 12:1–2, NEB).*

CHRISTIAN LEARNING AS ENABLEMENT

The Christian life is more than a remote moment of justification, or even a series of events which, when added together, result in what we refer to as sanctification. The Christian life is lived under the reality of God's continuing action in history.

Though sanctification is rooted in the accomplished fact of our salvation, it represents a goal to be completed. Sanctification, then, is both a present reality and the goal of God's work in man. Others have labored and learned, and we enter into the fruit of their labor.

How is one enabled to enter into the labor of God? Paul declares that "where the Spirit of the Lord is, there is freedom. And we all, with unveiled face, beholding the glory of the Lord, are being changed into his likeness from one degree of glory to another" (2 Cor. 3:17–18, RSV).

In other words, the Christian life is a continuous learning experience in which the learner is being shaped by God's workmanship. God enables us to become ourselves. This process of *becoming* takes place in several ways.

Growth comes when the believer intentionally decides to pat-

---

* *The New English Bible, New Testament,* © copyright The Delegates of the Oxford University Press and the Syndics of the Cambridge University Press 1961. All quotations used by permission.

tern or copy his life after the Son of God. This is more than a parrot-like copying of Christ. Rather, this patterning or modeling represents a response to love in action. The claim of Christ upon our lives is internalized. Paul, in his second Corinthian letter, indicates that it is the love of Christ which motivates him.

Learning and growth for the Christian, then, is rooted in the constraint of love. In New Testament terms, the motivation for learning is the love of God revealed in Jesus Christ.

The courage to change, repent, and grow is made possible for the Christian adult leader as he continues to rediscover his identity in Christ. This is a day-by-day process. There can be no "once for all" attitude regarding *our* relationship to God in Jesus Christ.

It is in Christ that we are able to discover each day who we are and what we were intended to be. Herein lies the answer for all those of our time who have problems of self-identity. The process of coming to learn one's own identity involves the encounter with ourselves as well as becoming what we already are in Christ.

If Christ is to be formed in us, we as learners must be willing to open ourselves to change. The value of the true Christian community is that it provides a place where Christ's learners can participate and try out new behaviors. The job of self-examination and renewal is sustained as we participate in the community of believers where abiding Christian values operate.

A good word needs to be said for the church! We are all aware that the church is not always what God intended it to be. The answer to the problem, however, is not found in bypassing membership in the body of Christ. Rather, the believer should use his energy and effort to assist the church in being what God intended it to be. God's divinely ordained body can be a prophetic community which in its life and work presents a bold witness to the power of God to transform every human problem.

Are you allowing God through Christ to conform you each day to his image? To be in Christ is to have found the center of authority in Christ. Adult education and learning cannot be complete unless it resolves this question. The adult learner must personally discover the answer to this question each day.

If life can be so characterized, then we are enabled to come at last to that "... mature manhood, measured by nothing less than the full stature of Christ" (Eph. 4:13, NEB).

Useful Assumptions About Adult Learning

Thus far, we have dealt with adult learning from a biblical and theological perspective. In addition, the concept of lifelong learning has been stressed.

It seems abundantly clear that adults can and do learn. Furthermore, this learning takes place in all of life's experiences. And, finally, adult learning is incomplete unless it begins and continues as a dynamic relationship with the living Christ.

However, it is one thing to know that adults can and do learn. To know how this learning takes place or to understand the characteristics of the adult learner and the adult learning situation is something else.

Robert Clemmons insists that: "If an approach to adult learning is to be valid, its basic assumption needs to be checked with the best that we know in the social sciences and in biblical, theological, and ethical thought. . . . " [2] The purpose of this section of the chapter is to view Christian adult learning in light of sound principles of learning verified by education and the social sciences.

Teachers and leaders of adults must be able to understand the process of adult learning and to perceive what is happening to adults so that they may lead them in their development.

1. *Principles concerning the ways adults learn.*—Anyone who has worked with learning groups is quick to discover certain principles that characterize the uniqueness of that situation. The following ideas are illustrative:

(1) *Adults learn through their own initiative.*—It won't take you long as a leader to discover that you cannot learn for the

learner. You may guide, encourage, excite, stimulate, model the role, and motivate him, but ultimately *he* must do the learning! Learning cannot be handed to the adult to be put on as if it were a coat.

There is an older misconception concerning learning, sometimes called "the hole in the head" theory of learning. The idea was that a teacher could pour into the head of the learner all that he needed to know and learning would result.

Learning, however, takes place from *within* the learner. All the teaching, preaching, and attempts at training will prove ineffective unless the individual does something about it. Learning is directly dependent upon the measure of personal energy exerted by the learner.

(2) *Adults learn from their identification with groups.*—In adult life, we are continuously brought together in groups. Much of adult teaching is related to the ways in which we perceive people and enable them to work together.

An adult rarely associates himself with a learning group or experience without some personal reason. It must be abundantly clear to the learner that certain values and rewards will accrue as the result of his learning effort. The more an individual comprehends the personal reasons and need for learning, the more he associates himself with the activity.

The closer he may be led to identify himself with various church learning groups, the greater the growth and learning resulting from that identification. A first step in this identification process is to lead the adult to become a member of the group. The more he commits himself to the purpose and objectives of the group, the more he profits and is benefited.

The implication of this principle is that adults want to know the "why" of learning. When you attempt to enlist them in a learning activity, the first question they ask is, "Why is it important and of what value will this learning be to me?" The thoroughness with which the learning leader addresses himself to this question will determine the intensity of the learner's involvement and interest.

(3) *Adults learn as the result of growth in knowledge.*—Building an adequate cognitive structure of ideas and concepts is a basic part of learning for all adults. It is for this very reason that the church provides such programs of learning as Bible study, member and leader training, missionary education, and music.

All adults are candidates for more knowledge. In fact, knowledge is basic to all mental and spiritual growth. A sensitive learning leader will be anxious to help the learner find access to areas of new knowledge and information.

Some early advice was given to me by a most helpful Christian counselor. He suggested that I should learn some new Bible knowledge every day. The believer is admonished to "grow in grace, and in the knowledge of our Lord and Saviour Jesus Christ" (2 Peter 3:18).

The mastery of word symbols and meanings in the Bible or of the Christian heritage is an important part of interpreting the relationships of life. One of the hazards of adult learning that we face at the cognitive level is the tendency of persons to become fixed in their thought systems. When adults are threatened and feel insecure about life, a rigid cognitive style begins to develop.

That is why it is so important that adults continue in daily learning. The verses of God's Word should "pop" out from the pages. *New* excitement should spring forth within the learner as he enters into communication with the content of the curriculum and with other persons.

(4) *Adults learn from their own creative participation.*—The various encounters of the Christian life involve the acquiring of subjective meanings and their personal expressions. This means moving beyond objective truth. Not only must the learner "learn about the Bible," but he must appropriate it and make it his own. Learning comes to adults as they become "doers of the word, and not hearers only" (James 1:22). The teachings of the New Testament make it very clear that Christian knowledge is incomplete until it performs that which it knows. Knowledge and action fit together like hand and glove. Knowledge should pro-

duce action, and likewise action or involvement with life reveals the need for more knowledge.

The significance of this principle should be self-evident. The "sit still while I instil" philosophy needs to be eradicated in church learning groups. There is more to learning than giving people information or stamping the right answers into their minds.

Sharing or imparting information may represent a legitimate part of the learning experience, but the ultimate test of learning is the ability to use knowledge.

(5) *Adults learn from their associations with the leader.*—The mystery of influence of one person over another is better known than understood. Leaders of adults must be very aware of this dimension of adult learning.

Adults, by nature, are very discriminating. It is more important that you be accepted for what you are as a person than for your knowledge or skill in leading. If the life you model before the learner is hypocritical, it is doubtful that you will be able to help the learner.

On the other hand, can you recall from your own experience those strong and courageous persons who have greatly influenced your life? These were probably not self-willed and exploitative persons. Rather, they could be characterized by their self-giving and empathetic concern for the learner.

(6) *Adults learn by handling life problems and tasks.*—Much learning in the Christian community takes place on a feeling basis. Most adults derive status in life from the roles they perform. These roles are primarily related to the expectations of life that emerge from the period of life in which a person finds himself. In other words, each stage of adult life contains certain unique performance tasks that must be negotiated.

Adults find acceptance in society in relation to the manner in which life tasks are performed. Very often, problems and difficulties attend life tasks. Temptations, crises, disturbances, and frustrations cannot be avoided. These experiences bring either defeat or victory. Life's difficulties either mellow a person and bring him closer to the will of God, or they defeat him and take him further from the ultimate will of God for his life.

Proper guidance from others in the learning fellowship will assist the adult in overcoming problems and difficulties. If the adult has help and is able to handle these difficulties, then his life is strengthened. Through these kinds of experiences he learns.

The learning fellowship becomes a true representation of the body of Christ when it offers itself redemptively to persons in need. There is, indeed, a close relationship between ministry and learning.

2. *Characteristics of adult learners and the learning situation.*—Too often the church has approached adult learning as if it were an extension of childhood and youth education. Adults are not just grown-up children. We have problems to solve that are altogether different from those of children and youth. Therefore, it is important for the learning leader to understand how the adult learner differs from other learners.

(1) *Adults need to feel that the learning objectives are their own.*—Telling adults the learning content is theirs is one thing. Assisting them to discover real learning needs and cooperatively planning experiences based on those needs is something else. The leader makes a tragic mistake when he *imposes* learning content upon the learner.

(2) *Adults prefer to select what they will learn.*—Adults do not always choose to learn that which is best for them. However, because they have a rich background of experience, they can be trusted to make wiser decisions than can children and youth. It is paradoxical that in many churches children have freedom to select the types of learning activities with which they will identify in a given unit of study. On the other hand, the adult must sit passively and patiently endure the monologic experience that was planned for him. The more the adult learner can be given a voice in the planning of learning, the greater will be his interest in the activity.

(3) *Adult learners are more problem-centered in their orien-*

tation to learning.—Adults, typically, enter into learning situations to find help for life problems. Whereas children and young people may learn "subjects" anticipating some future goal or end, the adult is a "doer" and he wants help now. For example, a young person might study marriage and parenthood, anticipating these future roles. His interest and motivation for such a study will be entirely different when he becomes a parent.

The implication of this characteristic is that adults come to learning with the intent of much more immediate application than youth. If the adult comes to your group and finds little that is of personal relevance, he may not return.

(4) *Adult learners have more to contribute to a learning experience than do children and youth.*—Adults usually have had more experiences because they have lived longer than children. As Paul Bergevin suggests:

> . . . they [adults] have had different kinds of experiences; and they usually interpret their experiences differently than children. While many of these situations may not have contributed to the maturation of the adults, they nevertheless exist and must be considered with care and caution. Some experiences contribute to our well-being and the civilizing process, and others could destroy both.[3]

The Christian adult learning leader must be sensitive to the uses to which individual experiences can be put.

(5) *Adult learners are both dependent and independent.*— Innately, adults want to do for themselves, yet they often depend on others. The wise leader will direct the energies of the learner toward a more self-reliant stance.

In a church where I served, a retired carpenter was a member of an older adult group. He was faithful to his church. Every time the doors of the church were open, he was there. Yet, because he was a timid man, his faithful attendance was the extent of his participation. For example, he refused to pray or read publicly. Seldom did he participate verbally in the class sessions.

The wise teacher of his Sunday School class recognized that

there was much this man could contribute which could heighten his participation level. He enlisted the retired carpenter to prepare a learning aid that would be used in connection with a unit of study. The learning aid was to be a relief map of the Palestinian area.

The learner agreed to make the map but insisted that the teacher would need to help him. Teacher and pupil went together to the church library where resource information was secured. The aid was prepared and was used by the learning group. That, however, is not the main point of the story.

While in the church library securing information for his assignment, the retired carpenter met a new friend: the world of books! He had time for reading and became interested in reading. He later admitted that he had not read a book through in more than twenty years. He had read newspapers and magazines but had not read a book.

He developed an enthusiasm for reading and in less than a year's time had read more than thirty books. What do you think happened to the participation level of this man in his Sunday School class? What happens when you get excited about a new idea? You want to share it! Such was the case with this man. Overnight, seemingly, this man changed! He became more confident of himself and more self-reliant. All of this happened because a teacher was sensitive to the "dependent-independent" characteristic of the learner.

Notice that in this experience, the leader asked the learner to do something that he at the moment could do. The performance at that level resulted in more involved participation.

(6) *Adult learners tend to withdraw from situations that threaten their self-image.*—It has been pointed out that an adult is primarily a "doer" or "producer," whereas a child or youth's primary role is that of student.

The adult's image of himself is derived primarily from his participation in outside activities. He brings this image of himself with him to the learning experience. If he is looked down upon, or treated as a child, he finds his image of himself as a responsible adult threatened and more than likely will withdraw from that situation.

(7) *Adults need help in practicing what they learn.*—Nothing will be more important to the learner than the opportunity provided him to practice what he learns.

Twentieth-century education has stressed participation and personal discovery. The new approaches to teaching, such as "team teaching," call attention to the need for the group to become a production team.

In a modern world where man cannot even pretend to know the answers, learning based on predetermined solutions to problems is obsolete. Learning must take place in the arena and events of life. When this happens, teachers will not be giving answers to unasked questions.

Practice also helps the learner reinforce that knowledge which is learned. In addition, skills related to knowledge cannot be developed apart from practice. Have you ever come away from a study in personal soul-winning feeling frustrated because the teacher told you how to do it? Think how much more related and meaningful the learning would have been had you been given the personal opportunity to practice the principles you had learned.

(8) *Adult learning is limited by self-imposed restraints.*—The tendency for some adults to try to hold to established patterns of behavior shows itself clearly in church learning activities. They sometimes find new ideas and challenging experiences disturbing. These new experiences and ideas conflict with their desire to keep things like they are. These are the adults who would rather learn about what they already know than to confront the possibility of change.

Sometimes adults express this threat or fear by saying, "I am too old to learn that," or "What good would that do me?" These self-imposed restraints represent the greatest barriers to Christian adult education. Basic to any attempt at adult education in the church is the profound belief that a person need not be "set in his ways." However, you as the leader must be able to identify these negative traits.

To summarize this section of the chapter, evaluate the following statements. These statements, given by a noted adult educator, serve to summarize the uniqueness of adult learner characteristics. As you evaluate these statements, react to them in terms of adults in the group which you lead or of which you are a member.

1. Adults come to learning programs with a more definite "set" than children;
2. Adult personality is more permanently fixed for good or ill;
3. Adults have more emotional connections with words, situations, institutions, and people than do children;
4. Many adults bring negative feelings with them to the learning situation because they resent authority;
5. Adults are more under the burden of certain stereotypes like personality and belief than are children, who are in a more formative stage of development;
6. Inadequacy and failure is more likely to be in the forefront of an adult's mind than of a child's;
7. The adult may see new learning as more of a threat to the balance and integration he has attempted to achieve;
8. Most adults must rather quickly see more relevance and immediacy of application than children do;
9. A group of, say, fifteen adults will usually have more variations in skills, interests, experience, and education than a similar group of children. They might be considered more highly differentiated;
10. Adult attitudes are difficult to change. If learning is not shaped to fit, any change will be forgotten or rejected;
11. Learners always look at situations, not necessarily as they are, but as they perceive them to be.[4]

2

Examining the Role
of the
Learning Leader

HENRY ADAMS, a noted educator of the first part of this century, wrote, "A teacher affects eternity; he can never tell where his influence stops." The range of a teacher's influence is beyond calculated measurement.

Annie Sullivan's life as the teacher of Helen Keller is an immortal and moving oration. William Gibson, in his play *The Miracle Worker*, describes how a tormented, vicious, beastly—but intelligent—child was released from the prison of her body to enter the hall of fame because of the dedication and loving concern of her teacher. Apparently, Annie wrestled with Helen just as Jacob of old wrestled with the "man."

Helen Keller's teacher was determined to receive a blessing—the blessing of Helen's response to love. Her love kindled love in Helen's heart and opened the door to further excitement and growth in learning. Together teacher and learner lived, probing the deeper meanings of life, seeking answers to the human predicament. Their personal discovery became an exciting experience which transformed both of them.

Somewhere at the heart of this beautiful relationship is to be found the essential meaning of teaching. Annie Sullivan became a "change agent."

MISCONCEPTIONS CONCERNING THE ROLE OF A LEARNING LEADER

From what sources have you derived your understanding of the role of a learning leader? Most of us who are teachers-in-training will be more inclined to teach as we were and are taught. It will prove fruitful for us to take a look at the several models of learning leaders that may exist in the minds of some people.

Some teachers have taken their model from the *preacher in the pulpit*. His was the "priesthood of knowledge," his the "litany of the lesson." If the pupils were "miserable sinners," there was hope for them through following good advice. It was for them to listen and learn. Not only is this poor theology, but it is weak learning theory as well.

For some, their model of teaching has been derived from the *schoolmaster behind the sacred seat of learning*. Pupils were expected to sit quietly while the teacher transmitted information and facts to them. The learner was considered nothing more than a "jug to be filled." The learner, it was thought, came to the classroom with an empty slate hung around his neck on which he said to the teacher, "Write!"

Others of us may have developed our model of the learning leader from that of the *actor*. Such a concept may view the teacher as a solo performer. He rehearses the script, manipulates and utilizes the props, and dramatically presents his lines to the audience.

These are absurd examples, and yet they are fairly accurate representations of teachers held by some people.

THE ROLE OF THE LEARNING LEADER

There is a sense in which the traditional word "teacher" leaves something to be desired. There is nothing essentially wrong with the term "teacher." However, some of the negative factors associated with the term may have caused us to develop warped concepts about what a teacher is and does. The word "teacher" is almost a sacred term among our Baptist people. And yet the word itself is inadequate.

What is needed is a noun that means "he-who-assists-learning-to-happen." The teacher is in fact a change agent. He helps produce change and growth in the lives of learners.

Great teachers of history have been this kind of catalytic agents. The priests, seers, wise men, prophets, scribes, and rabbis of the Old Testament were such change agents. The Aaronic priests served to guide Israel in ways of right living. They encouraged the people in the doing of right and decried folly. They pointed out the inevitable consequences of wickedness and commended righteousness.

The judges and prophets devoted the greater portion of their time to the social problems of the day. They used their energies to assist with individual and national problems. To the prophets was given inspired understanding of God's purpose to send the Messiah, and it was their business as helpers to prepare the way.

The master teacher of all ages was Jesus Christ, who came "to give light to them that sit in darkness . . . , to guide our feet into the way of peace" (Luke 1:79). Gaines S. Dobbins has stated that Jesus' supreme greatness is to be found not just in what he said but in what he was, and what he produced in the lives of his learners or disciples.

As our Lord went about doing the work of his earthly ministry, he took his disciples with him so they too could learn to follow his example. He lived and learned with his pupils.

He commissioned the seventy to go "two and two before his face into every city and place, whither he himself would come" (Luke 10:1). His personal guidance in doing what he taught them enabled them to develop leadership skills. In order to produce such growth and change in the lives of his learners, Jesus utilized a multifaceted approach to teaching.

To study the lives of these and other great teachers of history is to discover that teaching is far more than classroom performance.

Leading in learning is a multidimensional role. At the beginning of a new church year, hundreds of new teachers walk into adult classrooms to face their students. These leaders are confronted with the same problem that has challenged educators for many centuries—how to teach.

These leaders must not only be adept as instructors, but they must be eager learners themselves. Learning is such a complicated affair that no one ever fully masters it. One needs to be constantly alert for new manifestations. Keeping up-to-date in regard to learning is comparable only with keeping up-to-date in regard to medical practice.

If the teacher is himself a learner, this will mean periodic changes in teaching style or performance. The Adult teacher, more than anybody else, is obligated to be well-informed in regard to the latest developments in teaching technique. One of the purposes of this book is to assist you at this very point.

In addition to being learners, leaders of Adults must be good listeners, counselors, and confidants. Such a role demands the development of skills in human relations. To live and learn with the learner requires you to study the nature of human nature and to develop an awareness of adult psychology.°

Such a multidimensional role requires genuine dedication to the principles of educational excellence. One can begin to learn about this task of being a learning leader by trying to understand the meaning of the word "education." Unfortunately, too many people have the erroneous impression that the word is from the Latin *educo, educare,* meaning "to draw forth" or "to lead out of."

To carry that concept into the classroom would mean that the adult learning leader is one who elicits answers in much the same way that a dentist extracts teeth. But a teacher is not a

---

° A companion book to this text was written to aid you in your understanding of adult psychology. It is entitled *Understanding Adults,* by Lucien Coleman, Jr., (Nashville: Convention Press, 1969).

dentist, and education should not be thought of only from that viewpoint.

Education, and especially Christian education, is more than merely asking students to give back what the teacher has presented. "Education" truly means to nourish (from the Latin *educo, educare*). Therefore, one might envision the role of the teacher as similar to that of a mother giving nourishment to a child.

Teachers must nourish their students with sound principles of learning. They must help learners learn how to learn. Teachers must nourish their students with the richness of content which is personally discovered and practiced by both teacher and student. Teachers must nourish their students with a concrete example of Christian living. It is a trite but true statement that more is *caught* than *taught*.

Is it clear to you that teaching represents more than what you say in the classroom? Once it is agreed that teaching is not merely an encyclopedic transmittal of facts, this vital question still remains: *How* may one most effectively teach the values, concepts, and skills of the Christian life?

Just as there is no one best road to Loch Lomond, so too there is no single success formula for teachers to follow. Opinions vary as to whether teachers are "born" or "made." It is the contention here that teachers cannot be classified in either category exclusively. Certain innate skills and talents are helpful, but such ability must be thoroughly developed and complimented with the knowledge of "how to teach" before you can be truly successful in the performance of your role.

TEACHING AND LEARNING

In chapter 1, a definition of learning was suggested. Can you write down this definition from memory? If not, look back to the definition, then write it on the margin of this page.

Learning represents a behavioral change that takes place within the learner. Behavioral change can represent any expression of which the learner is capable. Such things as accumulation of new biblical knowledge, the alteration or addition of an attitude, or the development of a new skill are examples of behavioral change.

Teaching, then, is causing change to occur within the learner. Perhaps we should attempt, at this point, to work out a suitable definition of teaching. Lay this book down and formulate in your own mind such a definition. When you have it clearly in mind, write it down in the margin of the page under the definition of learning. Allow the ideas presented thus far to stimulate your thinking.

Just as there have been thousands of books written on the subject of teaching, there are as many definitions of teaching. We can learn from them all. But each learning leader must finally adopt his own definition of teaching, which will become his philosophy of teaching.

From research and study, the following definition represents my present concept of Christian teaching: *Christian teaching is guiding, stimulating, and motivating the learner in his own personal discovery and practice of biblical truths and concepts.* How do you react to this definition? Compare it with your own.

Implicit in this definition are several major principles:

1. The definition assumes that the teacher can't learn for the learner.
2. The definition reflects what has been said about the role of the leader as a catalytic agent.
3. The definition calls attention to the equipping and guidance role of the teacher.
4. The definition views the learner as being actively involved and participating in the activities of learning.
5. The definition focuses upon the personal quality of learning.
6. The definition asserts that a chief goal of teaching is helping pupils to think and form their own convictions. The goal of teaching is never concensus or agreement. Rather,

the purpose of the teacher is to stimulate the thought processes of the learner.

7. The definition concludes that learning and teaching are incomplete until knowledge can be put to work.

8. The definition delineates the multifaceted role of the leader. He is viewed as a director of learning (working with groups), a counselor (emphasizing concern for the individual), a manager (arranging resources and conditions for effective learning), and guide (nurturing the learner in his quest for Christian maturity).

9. The definition acknowledges the doctrine of the priesthood of the believer. Emphasis is upon personal discovery.

10. The definition welcomes the operation and work of the Holy Spirit. The dynamic force of the Holy Spirit enables individual adult learners to be "instructed in righteousness."

Learning leaders in Bible study, church member training, missionary education, and music education programs do essentially the same kind of work. Content, curriculum resources, aims or instructional objectives, or group structure may vary. But the role of the leader does not vary. His job is to help the learner to read, think, and respond to biblically based content. He works to assist the learner in learning to use what he has learned.

MASTERING THE LOGIC OF THE TEACHING PROCESS

There is a logical process in the teaching-learning transaction. These patterns of logic, once mastered, will enable you to sharpen the quality and effectiveness of your leadership with the group.

In a consideration of a comprehensive teaching process, the following is a suggested model.

1. Identify the desired learning outcomes for a unit of study.

2. Specify the objectives of instruction for learning sessions of the unit.

3. Analyze the learners and make decisions about their present relationship to the content.
4. Select information and materials and make decisions about methods.
5. Involve the learners in activities presumed to lead to learning.
6. Direct and guide the learning activities.
7. Provide situations or simulations for using the learnings.
8. Evaluate the outcomes of the learning process.

In actual practice, the process may not be this systematic. A number of these activities may go on concurrently, earlier decisions may be revised, or blind alleys may force a new plan. Some evaluation will take place throughout the process.

For some adult leaders, little of this model is followed consciously. Classroom activities are represented by default rather than planning. Some teachers may "identify the desired learning outcome" by predeciding the material to be covered and assuming that the learner will "learn" the material without working through what is meant by "learning the material."

Some of us who teach or lead may be tempted to "analyze" learner needs and make decisions about their readiness by assuming certain common and average characteristics of the group. Lesson information and materials are often selected by using the prescribed content as it appears in the literature, and methods are frequently selected on the basis of tradition or our familiarity with their use.

Let us examine each step of the model to see its possible range, and draw some implications about possible levels of quality in teaching.

1. *Identify the desired learning outcomes for a unit of study.* —A first step in planning to teach a unit of study is to "get the feel" of the nature of the content. This is achieved by considering all the lessons, biblical material, bibliography, supplementary resources, and related material of the unit.

Once you have developed an understanding of the nature of

the unit, you are ready to write a unit aim and tentative lesson aim or goals. The *unit aim* is a larger purpose that is supported by two or more lessons that naturally fit together. One lesson period is all too brief a time in which to accomplish a major objective. A group of lessons fit together to interpret and clarify a major idea or theme.

John Sisemore points out that "When the teacher recognizes the learning goals in the units, they become a foundation on which he builds a superstructure of learning. Otherwise, there is simply a disjointed, hodgepodge of miscellaneous material. Unit aims are the key to learning goals." [1]

2. *Specify the objectives of instruction for learning sessions of the unit.*—The *lesson aim* or goal is a more specific statement that identifies what the learner will be able to do when he demonstrates that he has learned. A lesson aim should always represent some desired behavioral change. To determine the lesson aim is to focus the priority content and direction of the lesson. Chapter 3 will explain how to determine and write learning aims or goals.

To identify outcomes of learning is to consider the behavior of the learner as open to potential change in three dimensions: the *cognitive* or that of knowledge, the *affective* or that of attitude, and the *active* or that of skill development. To state this in another way, we could say that it affects a person's thinking, his feeling, and his doing. Actual outcomes may represent a blend of the three.

***Cognitive outcomes.*—**Sometimes the Adult teacher feels that learners should know more, have more information, develop new concepts, recognize things that were previously unknown, and be able to recall information presented in the class. The teacher may want learners to increase the complexities of their understandings, to expand existing concepts into wider understandings, to understand more of the implications of a topic. He may want changes to occur in their modes of thinking so that learners become more imaginative and think more analytically or creatively.

The teacher is using a knowledge aim, according to Findley Edge, "if the dominant purpose of the teacher is to lead the class in a logical, systematic, intensive study of a body of knowledge and to lead to a mastery of that knowledge."[2]

An example of a cognitive outcome would be an aim statement like the following: *At the end of this session, learners should be able to reconstruct the major events of Passion Week and explain the significance of each.*

Affective outcomes.—The affective outcomes of learning have to do with the way the learners feel, their emotional reactions, and motivational tendencies. As an outcome of the teaching situation, how should pupils feel about race relations, ethical problems, and opportunities for Christian ministry? What kind of emotional responses do we want concerning such Christian concepts of love, justice, mercy, and long-suffering?

How do we expect learners to feel about themselves and others and about their relationships and responsibilities to others? Every aspect of teaching that is related to how a learner feels about a truth is very significant, because feelings and emotions play a vital part in learning.

Affective outcomes of learning are directed toward a much deeper level of learning than cognitive outcomes. And yet, as Sisemore reminds us, "any feeling lessens as time dulls the memory of the response. Good teaching requires a reasonable appeal to emotion, but permanency in learning is not easily obtained with an inspirational [affective] aim alone."[3]

A typical affective or inspirational aim or goal might be: *At the end of this session, learners should be able to appreciate and value more highly the importance of mission activity in Biafra.*

Active outcomes.—When we speak of the active dimension of learning, we are thinking of skills in doing things, the carrying on of actual observable behavior—writing, speaking, singing, leading.

The problem becomes complicated here because we want two levels of action as outcomes of teaching, and it is important to distinguish between the two.

First, we may want to develop a skill itself, such as learning to make a hospital visit or learning to verbalize the gospel as a Christian witness to an unsaved adult. Secondly, we may want to use the act as evidence of cognitive and affective learning.

When an adult gives an appropriate response to a test item, as in a post-test for a unit of study, he has demonstrated only the skill of producing a particular verbal behavior under a stimulus situation. This does indicate a certain level of learning proficiency. The same could be said of reciting verses or passages of Scripture "by heart." These activities may or may not indicate genuine understanding and appreciation of the content. But when the learner can use memorized verses of Scripture in a soul-winning interview, or remember and apply learned principles of how to visit the sick in a hospital visit, he learns at a much deeper level. Many experts in the field of education claim that cognitive and affective outcomes are noticeably improved by the initial focus on active outcomes.

This suggests that a greater portion of your teaching energies with adults ought to be directed toward skill development. Many informed and intelligent Baptist people are saying, "For years we have studied the 'what' of the Christian life. Give us a chance to 'do!'" The mission action groups of the missionary education programs seek to put the learner into the arena of acting and doing, the performance of which leads to further motivation in cognitive and affective learning.

An illustration of an active outcome of learning might be: *At the end of this session, learners, using selected verses from the book of Romans, should be able to tell someone else how to receive Christ as personal Saviour.*

What kind of aim will you use in a given learning situation? This will depend on several factors. In summary, we agree with Rice Pierce, who states that "It may be . . . that your class members' deepest spiritual concern will help you to decide which type of aim to use in planning for a given session." Your study of the next chapter will strengthen your understanding and skills in determining learning outcomes.

3. *Analyze the learners and make decisions about their present relationship to the content.*—Having some idea of the expected outcomes, the hoped-for changes within the learner which will come forth from teaching activities, the learning leader must also have some idea of the present characteristics of the learners he is leading.

A great deal of time and energy is wasted by teachers who do not know learners well enough to identify their present status before attempting to change or improve it.

How does a teacher analyze a group of learners? Consider the following:

1. Benefit from a general knowledge about the psychology of adult learners.
2. Use existing concepts about average or normal behavior and its range.
3. Observe and listen to adults in your group in order to compare them to these concepts.
4. Note individual differences among adults, especially those that may be helpful or harmful to the planned learning activities.
5. Engage in specific measurement procedure such as pre-tests, post-tests, directed discussions, interest inventories, leader-learner planning, or the gathering of information on individual pupils.

A helpful "Pupil Information Instrument" is given below to serve as a guide for leaders who want to know certain types of information about adult learners. You will want to add to the instrument questions of your own which are not included here. The instrument is adapted from one suggested by Edge.[4]

1. GENERAL INFORMATION

Name _____ Address _____

Telephone no. _____ Birth date _____ Age ____

Sex _____

Department _____ Class _____

2. HOME LIFE

Father's name? _____ Occupation _____

Church member? _____ Where? _____

Sunday School member? _____

Mother's name _____ Occupation? _____

Church member: _____ Where? _____

Sunday School member? _____

What is the economic status of the family? _____

Do they have family worship? _____

Is there an atmosphere of love and happiness in the home? _____

What are the attitudes of the father and mother toward the children? _____

Do they display keen interest in the children? _____

Would the neighborhood be rated as above average, average, or below average? _____ What unfavorable influences are there in the community?

_____

What favorable influences? _____

3. COMPANIONSHIPS

Does he have few or many friends? _____ Does he make friends readily or slowly? _____ Is he concerned more with giving or getting in friendships? _____ Is the influence of his companions in general helpful or harmful? _____ Is he primarily a leader or a follower? _____ Does he choose his companions from the same social level or otherwise? _____ From church circle or elsewhere? _____ What evidences of growth in capacity for Christian friendship? _____

4. TEMPERAMENT AND DISPOSITION

Is he primarily self-centered or interested in others? _____ Is he sensitive? _____ Is he good-natured? _____ Is he dependent or independent? _____ Does he like notice and prominence? _____ Does he shrink from responsibility? _____ Is he more aggressive or timid? _____ Does he have a happy outlook on life? _____ Does he have a healthy attitude toward religion? _____ Does he anger easily? _____ Does he control his temper and emotions? _____ Is he able to reason?'_____ Does he have a cheerful disposition? _____ Is he tolerant of others? _____

5. RECREATION AND HOBBIES

What is his favorite recreational activity? _____ What other types of recreation does he engage in? _____ How much time does he have for recreation? _____ Does he follow sports primarily as a spectator? _____ What hobbies does he have? _____ What type of social life does he engage in? _____ Is he more of a leader or a follower in recreation? _____

6. SPECIAL INTERESTS AND ABILITIES

Indicate interests that center chiefly about the home. _____ About work. _____ About school. _____ About intellectual activities. _____ About social activities. _____ Indicate his interest in the home. _____ His interest in money-making. _____ His interest in crafts. _____ Arts. _____ Music. _____ What are his talents? _____ How is he using them? _____ Does he need help in developing them? _____ What is his attitude toward his talents? _____ Is he afraid of criticism? _____

7. RELIGIOUS LIFE

Is he a Christian? _____ Church member? _____ What services of the church does he attend? _____ What services seem most to appeal to him? _____ In what organized activities of the church does he take part? _____ Is he interested in or indifferent to Bible study? _____ Is he interested in or indifferent to his church? _____ Is his religion an annoyance, a duty, a habit, or a source of joy? _____ Is his religion a growing, developing part of his life? _____ Does he put into practice what he learns in Sunday School and church? _____ Is he interested in missions? _____ Does he seek to enlist others? _____ What is his attitude toward stewardship? _____ Is he a personal witness? _____

It is very evident that successful teaching is more likely to occur when leaders of the learning situation know their learners intimately and teach them how, in light of their needs, to appropriate Christian concepts and ideals into life's experiences.

4. *Select information and materials and make decisions about methods.*—The denominationally prepared and produced materials serve as a rich foundation for adult learning experiences in Southern Baptist churches. Churches and leaders are wise to use these materials. Not many churches or groups have the resources for producing curricular materials. In addition to the curriculum base developed in the literature, there are curriculum supplements and other recommended resources that should be carefully selected and used.

The learning leader must also make decisions about the methods to be used in bringing together the group and the materials. For example, should the material be presented orally, or by assigned readings, through demonstration, with audio-visual techniques, by the use of programed materials,* or teaching machines which may be available? How can you balance the various methods?

Chapters 4 and 5 relate entirely to the matter of selecting and using appropriate methods, and techniques of instruction. Your mastery of these chapters will build up your confidence in the use of methods.

Finally, this step includes the preparation of teaching aids and the arrangement of the room for learning. These factors may seem incidental to some and quite beneath the dignity of others.

The use of good learning aids will help you highlight the essential ideas of a learning session and will reinforce learning content. Such aids include chalkboards, charts, maps, graphs, object lessons, posters, projected aids, and many others.‡ Learning tends to be *more* dialogical and thinking is stimulated with the appropriate use of these devices.

Classroom arrangement will depend on the type method or methods you plan to use. Remember, however, that informal seating arrangements that allow eye contact and face-to-face involvement create a more productive mood than do settings where chairs are arranged in rows.

I personally prefer to be seated around a table. The position of the leader will be determined, for the most part, by the methods used. So, the teacher is comfortable and thus puts the learners at ease.

5. *Involve the learners in activities presumed to lead to learning.*—So far in this discussion we have not involved the learner, except as he provides data for teacher decisions. It is now time to think about involving learners in planned activities, which will result in their progress toward planned outcomes.

You, as leader, must create situations which will stimulate

---

* For a sample of programed material for Adults, secure *Developing Skills for Bible Interpretation,* Lucien E. Coleman, Jr. (See Bibliography.)

‡ For details and "how to," see *Tools for Teaching and Training* by LeRoy Ford. (See Bibliography.)

learners to listen, read, write, discuss, ask questions, perform tasks, solve problems, think critically, prepare learning aids and devices, and engage in other activity appropriate to the expected learning. Since learning depends upon what the learner does, motivating the class in active participation is vital.

6. *Direct and guide the learning activities.*—In this step of the teaching process, the learning leader utilizes the methods and materials he has planned to direct the continuing activities of learners. Control and direction of these activities is achieved through telling, assigning, explaining, demonstrating, encouraging, and giving instructions.

By observing, listening, and evaluating, the leader measures the progress of learners. Through making suggestions and introducing new or supplementary materials and activities, the leader gives continuous guidance to learning.

Many leaders of church learning groups view the instructional assignment as that which takes place in the classroom. Learners, therefore, very often have a fragmented view of church learning experiences. How unfortunate it is if learning is thought to end at the end of the last session and to begin again one week later. The directive leader seeks to tie group experiences together. One experience should build on and be related to another. Review provides for continuity and serves to reinforce that which is learned. In addition, planning for learning over an extended period will tend to obligate learners. The more committed and involved the learner is, the greater will be his interest in the study.

As you direct learning activities, be sensitive and alert to the "teachable moment." Some authors speak of the teachable moment and imply that the learning process is enhanced if the teacher performs a particular instructional act when the conditions are ripe for it. It is at this point that the Christian leader can trust and rely upon the Holy Spirit to provide guidance. These instructional acts cannot always be planned in advance. You may discover that the spontaneous Spirit-led, instructional act can represent the most creative and right thing you do.

7. *Provide situations or simulations for using learnings.*—It is

generally accepted by all educators that learning has long-range value if the learner has a chance to practice or use the new concepts, attitudes, and skills in situations beyond those in which they were learned. The leader, therefore, should provide opportunities for the learner to use his new knowledge.

Such opportunities may be provided by incorporating the use of previously learned material in plans for the next session; by encouraging its use in situations that have reality to the learner; or by providing limited practice opportunity.

Have you experienced the frustration of trying to deal with personal application of the lesson just as the closing bell is ringing? It may be that the budgeting of your teaching time was carelessly done. Or perhaps you need more time for your learning groups. (It is doubtful that you will get much done in an Adult group unless you have at least 45 minutes to an hour for the group or class time.) It may be that you didn't get to spend productive time in lesson application because you didn't plan to. The creative planning that you do with this step is vital to your effectiveness as a learning leader.

8. *Evaluate the outcomes of the learning process.*—The significance of evaluation cannot be overemphasized. Obviously, some continuous evaluation of learning goes on throughout the teaching-learning transaction. It may be on a very informal level, but it does take place.

You as the leader should learn, however, that structured evaluation can improve instruction immeasurably. Evaluation concerns itself with two chief areas. The first has to do with finding out if the desired or predicted outcomes have occurred. The second is concerned with how effectively the learning process was conducted.

Determining the extent to which learning outcomes are attained is by far the more important of the two. As a matter of fact, it is the best proof of effective teaching. Here the teacher should be concerned with discovering whether learners have changed as far as concepts, information, knowledge, or skills are concerned. Do they think differently? To what extent do they feel differently in relation to the content being studied? What can they do now that they could not do when they entered the classroom? Are these changes for the good?

In practice, most learning outcome evaluation that is made with church learning groups tends to check only the verbal behavior of learners. From either written or spoken responses, other types of behaviors are inferred, not measured directly. Sometimes the leader may rely too heavily upon spoken response as a clue to learning outcomes. It is true that changes in the level of class discussion can be taken to indicate change in interest and understanding.

However, a more concrete way of measuring cognitive outcomes is to utilize tests. A test may be either written or oral. It may be an objective test composed of short-answer questions such as true-false, matching, completion, or multiple choice questions. Or it may be a subjective test composed of essay-type questions. The last chapter of this book will give you more complete information on the use of tests.

The second type of evaluation is also important. All participants can share in judging how effective the learning process is and how it might be improved. Suggestions for this type of evaluation are also contained in the last chapter.

If the leader has been able to specify the learning objectives in behavioral terms during his initial planning, he is more likely to be able to evaluate the actual outcomes.

The Learning Leader Using a Plan

Mr. Bored parked his car in the church parking lot and hurried to his classroom. On the way he was heard to say, "Let me see, what shall I teach them this morning?" Needless to say, such indifference toward the learning leadership role is shocking and insulting to the Christian belief in the worth of an individual. No task is more sacred than that of teaching others. How sad that Mr. Bored had denied himself the joy of being excited and enthused by a noble purpose and the joy of doing a worthwhile task.

Good teaching is planned! The learning leader needs to know where he is going and how to get there. Some Adult leaders may seek the *how* before the *why*, thinking this to be the urgent need; but this approach lacks conviction and enthusiasm.

Each unit and session in the curriculum materials contains teaching or training procedures that are thoughtfully prepared. But despite these wonderful helps, teaching is haphazard until these plans become your plan. Not until you have thoroughly studied, prepared, and personalized instruction have you done your best. Of course, you can plan *not* to plan as Mr. Bored did. But remember: *the quality of planning will greatly determine the quality of instruction and, therefore, the quality of learning.*

Sisemore reinforces the importance of planning when he suggests that the Bible magnifies planning, planning rightly relates teaching to learning, planning introduces the long look in teaching, and planning improves the teacher's skill.

THREE TYPES OF PLANS

Whether you are a leader in the church's Bible teaching program, church member training program, missionary education program, or church music program, learning leadership is greatly facilitated by the use of a plan.

Here are three types of plans that are now used in Adult teaching. As you study these plans, notice that the logical steps in the teaching process are reflected in the plan.

PLAN I

(When you are teaching in a group setting.)

I. Direction of the lesson

   1. Date _____

   2. Unit title _____

3. Unit aim _____
4. Lesson title _____
5. Lesson passage _____
6. Central truth of lesson _____
7. Life needs of members _____
8. Lesson aim or goal _____

II. Procedure

1. Creating a readiness for learning.—*Use a device that is (1) centered in life, (2) interesting enough to catch attention immediately, (3) slanted to call for member response, and (4) suitable to lead directly into Bible study.*

2. Making Bible study purposeful.—*Use activities that (1) give the members something to discover or a problem to solve, (2) involve the members in actual Bible study, (3) survey the entire passage, (4) isolate important verses for special study, (5) locate the central truth, and (6) reveal new insights.*

3. Getting Bible truth into life.—*Use activities that (1) relate the applications to the aim, (2) are true to the Bible teaching, (3) are geared to getting members' suggestions, (4) are within the realm of members' interests, abilities, and needs, (5) commit the members to action, and (6) secure a definite carry-over activity.*

4. Motivating study of next lesson.—*Use activities that (1) arouse the members' curiosity, and (2) give them a purpose for study.*

PLAN 2

(When you are teaching one individual as a visitor-teacher.)

I. Determine direction of conversation

1. Lesson title _____
2. Bible passage _____
3. Member needs _____
4. Desired outcome for the conversation

_____

II. Select approach to conversation

1. Recount a learning experience you have had in Adult class to stimulate reaction by member. _____
2. Share an insight gained from personal study to encourage member to compare with the result of his study. _____
3. Raise a thought-provoking question to initiate a discussion with member.
4. Plan another means of creating interest.

_____

III. Involve member in conversation

1. Use questions found in members' quarterly.
2. Prepare a detailed study guide of questions to help member relate Bible truths to life needs. _____
3. Select a different translation of the Bible to clarify meaning of lesson passage. _____
4. Plan another means of involving member in conversation. _____

IV. Stimulate Bible study between visits

1. Guide a review of lesson subjects for the next month. _____
2. Explain the purpose of a unit of lessons.

_____

3. Lead member to select the lesson for the next conversation. _____

PLAN 3
(When you are leading a group in church member training activities.)

I. Determine appropriate aim

II. Relate session emphasis to unit

III. Select learning methods

IV. Select suitable aids

V. Plan follow-through activities

VI. Evaluate the results

Did you notice similarities in these plans? All three deal with aims, goals, methods, aids, and suggestions for application.

As a leader, don't feel that you must follow these plans verbatim. You can make variations or adaptions to fit your specialized needs. However, it is necessary that you develop and use a comprehensive plan. These suggested plans are for your use.

THE LEADER AS A PERSON

What you are as a person is more important than what you say. Adult learners are looking for a genuine, authentic kind of person to lead them. They easily detect the superficial and hypocritical. Therefore, you must be very sensitive to the depth of your life and the range of your influence. These qualities of life can never be fully appropriated, but they should be goals toward which personal growth is directed. Here are some desirable qualities for those who lead Adults:

A redeemed and growing learner.—Anyone who teaches Adults the meaning of the Christian life must himself be a Christian. The basic readiness for teaching lies in a person's faith. It is made up of his comprehension of the gospel, his conception of what the gospel means to him, and the sense of responsibility he feels about sharing it with others.

One who is to teach Adults must *know* what God has done and is doing for him. What he knows "for sure" will find its way into his teaching.

The story has been told of an actor and a minister who were with a group of close friends. The actor and the minister were both requested to quote the twenty-third Psalm. The actor did so perfectly, and his flawless presentation illicited applause from the group. Then the elderly minister quoted the psalm. His personal experience with the passage through many experiences of comforting others was clearly evident as he quoted it. So moving was the recital that his friends were in tears. After a hushed moment the actor blurted out, "I know the psalm, but you know the Shepherd of the psalm." Knowledge that is lived out is the most important kind for a teacher to possess.

A craftsman as well as an artist.—The mystery of leadership is better known than understood. In many respects, a teacher as leader in the classroom is like a scientist. He has a holy curiosity and an inquiring mind. He searches for truth wherever he can find it—in the Scriptures, in manuals, audiovisual aids, music, resource materials, and from resource persons. He uses his critical judgment to distinguish between evidence and interpretation, fact and fiction.

A successful leader is more than a scientist. He is an artist who goes beyond intelligence into the realm of wisdom and insight. The art of teaching cannot be taught to others; it must be personally cultivated. Artists tell us that the best art comes from the most difficult medium. We who attempt to teach seek to mold students. They can, at times, be a most difficult medium. But how rewarding to see growth, symmetry, and beauty develop within a learner. Someone has well said, "A student is not a vessel to be filled, but a lamp to be lighted." It takes an artist as well as a craftsman to develop such a finished product.

A person who is clear in speech.—This quality is predicated upon a responsive and alert mind. The leader's willingness to reason, think, and clearly express himself appeals to adult learners. One reason many adults drop out of the various learning activities of the church is because they are not challenged to think.

A good leader chooses words wisely, always using the more familiar ones and then gradually moving to the unfamiliar and more complex ones.

An imaginative and creative person.—The creative leader encourages self-expression and is glad when he receives a variety of views. A leader who encourages initiative and originality raises the attention level of the learner. Rapport develops as a result, transfusing strength and vitality.

The most creative teacher was Jesus. Jesus' example in this realm is inspiring to those who seek to lead in learning. Matthew's Gospel gives this account of Jesus' teaching: "And when he was come into his own country, he taught them in their synagogue, insomuch that they were astonished, and said, Whence hath this man this wisdom, and these mighty works?" (Matt. 13:54). John records the reaction of some of Jesus' hearers: "And the Jews marvelled, saying, How knoweth this man letters, having never learned?" (John 7:15).

Your creative techniques in teaching will arouse curiosity and interest. Refrain from the temptation of being clever for clever's sake. The novel idea, however, grabs the learner and moves him toward the desired outcome.

A researcher.—How would you classify yourself? Do you tend to be satisfied with your present knowledge? Are you hungry for discovering and exploring the new? Satisfaction may be most deadly. No matter how successful you may have been, you should be looking ahead to new adventures in learning.

Such is the spirit of the researcher. He desires a deeper understanding of the Christian life. He seeks to understand his world and his place in it. He "thirsts after righteousness."

To be a researcher is largely a matter of hard work. It means working on plans far enough in advance of a particular session that consulted resources can become a part of what one does. Enrichment materials are worthless unless they are researched and used.

Being a researcher will give the leader time to get needed help from other people, or to send for materials that may have to be ordered. It also makes possible time for advanced assignments, and for planning ways to arouse interest in what is ahead.

The willingness to investigate, explore, and do research will enhance your analytical and perceptual skills. These skills will provide an additional kind of authority for the leader as he interacts with students.

A person who is able to deal with conflict and controversy. —Anytime you bring a group of adults together there is the possibility of conflict and controversy. Adults are not alike; neither do they think alike. Few groups organize or continue to meet without running into conflicts of beliefs, of ideas, of feelings.

Controversy is more frequent today because so many of our long-accepted ideas are being challenged. Disputes in a group can weaken or strengthen the group, depending on how they are handled. Avoid putting yourself up as an authority. Authority is inherent in what you genuinely are, and not in what you say.

Doctrines and creeds express vividly and precisely the generalizations of final truth perceived in particular instances of life. These perceptions are usually formulated verbally and expressed through a coherent system of thought, then applied to life interpretations. These doctrinal expressions bring meaning to the values held by man. But creeds are derived from partial perception of the total truth and sometimes distort truth by overemphasis of the partial as being absolute.

Remember what Paul said in 1 Corinthians 13:12: "Now I know in part; but then shall I know even as also I am known." The ultimate authority for adult learning situations is the Bible.

But man's understanding and interpretation of it may be partial.

You, the leader, must help group members develop intellectual humility so that in the study situation there is respect for the convictions and beliefs of others. Each learner has a responsibility to help each other. The leader's attitude of openness and honesty will do much to relieve tension that develops as the result of controversy.*

A person who is open and available to members.—Learn to give yourself to group members. There is no room in the adult learning situation for a leader who is self-centered and selfish. The supreme sacrifice of leadership is the willingness to give your life away for the welfare and benefit of others.

Leading adults in learning should be thought of as sharing friendship with them seven days a week! One of the greatest gifts you can offer to the learner is that of your own friendship. If you become puzzled as to how you can unlock the doors of an adult's inner life, then try being a true friend.

You are not likely to develop the quality of openness unless you are also developing the power of love. Some teachers crave the *love of power*. The truly redemptive leader seeks to know the *power of love*. If you have a tendency to selfishly control, exploit, and dominate persons or situations, then read often, "Be kindly affectioned one to another with brotherly love; in honour preferring one another" (Rom. 12:10).

A person who is willing to work.—Working with adults is work! Not all workers are workers. Some who are elected by the church do nothing except make a token "tip of the hat" to their responsibilities.

By work I mean preparing to lead, learning and living with learners, attending worker planning meetings, visiting and witnessing, and faithfully living out the faith which you profess as a member of Christ's body. The willingness to perform these

---

* For more help, see *How to Deal with Controversial Issues,* William Pinson. (See Bibliography.)

functions precludes an enthusiastic commitment to a task which you interpret to be the will of God for your life.

Your spirit and willingness to work will make the difference. A dead, lifeless Adult group can be transformed by the glowing, going life of a committed worker.

CONCLUSION

In this chapter, we have sought to examine the role of a learning leader. Leadership is a magic word, a marvelous attainment. The price you pay for it is significant. Pay but a small price and the return is meager. Pay the supreme price and the reward is genius and immortality, for you will be used by the eternal God to put in the world redeemed adults who will shine as the stars forever.

3

Determining
Learning
Outcomes

FAR UP THE SLOPES of an Oregon mountain grew a tree which for many long years had survived the storms and fires. Finally, the time came when it was to be cut down. With the last clean cut of the saw, it fell to the ground and was rolled into a stream where it made its way toward the sawmill. Because of poor planning and inexperienced help, the workers at the mill were not able to stop the log. It swiftly rushed downward past the mill and its intended usefulness, eventually coming to the ocean. Here, in the ocean, the stormtossed waves locked it with other trees, brush, and debris. Finally, the whole mass became a waterlogged mountain of rotting waste.

One dark, foggy morning, the look-out of a ship enroute to a distant port gave the signal, "Danger ahead!" Engines were reversed, speed reduced, and the captain rushed to the bridge for observation. One look at the pile of debris on the surface of the water was enough to cause him to turn away with an expression of disgust on his face. He exclaimed, "Only driftwood! Full speed ahead!"

The world is quick to recognize driftwood, whether it be debris in the water or sloppy church educational programs.

How often have adults not related to church programs turned their backs on our apparent aimlessness and steamed "full speed ahead" in other directions? How many of our own people have we lost because those involved in the guidance of the educational work have been too busy or too negligent to recognize and deal adequately with the real needs of members?

The Need for Guided Learning Experiences

The rush and press of life today has affected church members. They are faced with many different demands for their time and energy. Some have withdrawn from Christian education and training simply because they felt their time spent at church was not a good investment for the results being obtained. Others continue in church programs but are unaware of any growth which they might be experiencing.

It is possible to develop specific aims for church learning programs. Learners know the degree to which these aims are being achieved. In the complex world of today, however, unguided experience cannot teach us, in the time available, what we need to know. For this reason, it is necessary to organize learning experiences in order to achieve faster and more accurately certain important objectives. Only as church members are guided to make every learning moment count can we hope to reach basic objectives. The organization and guidance of learning experiences starts with a careful statement of the objectives and goals involved.

Learning Outcomes

It is deceptively difficult to state learning outcomes so that they can be used in the best way possible. There are several vital factors that must be considered:

1. The relevance of the learning goal to the real needs of the learners.
2. The identification of the subject matter involved.
3. The expected behavior implied in the learning goal.
4. The value which the learner should place on the learning goal.
5. The conditions under which the learning goal is to be achieved.
6. The standards by which to determine the extent to which the learning goal has been reached.

As an illustration, the writer's learning goal for the reader is that:

> After reading this chapter
> and responding to the exercises,
> you will be **willing**
> and **able**
> to write a learning goal
> for a group under your own direction,
> using the description of the six factors listed above
> as a reference.

Note the six factors related below, together with the section of this learning goal which is being illustrated:

1. *Relevance to needs of learners*—"a group under your own direction"—The implication is that because you have a group for which you are responsible, you will recognize the need to acquire the skill of stating objectives and learning goals.
2. *Subject matter*—"learning goal"—This is the *what* of the goal. It identifies specifically the subject matter that is involved.
3. *Behavior*—"write"—When dealing with the learning goal (the subject matter), the action required is that the learner *write* his own unique communication.

4. *Value*—"willing"—This learning goal states that the learner will be willing to respond, rather than simply be passive or antagonistic to the idea.
5. *Conditions*—"After reading this chapter and responding to the exercises . . . using the description of the six factors listed above as a reference"—The conditions quoted describe the circumstances which are involved as the learning goal is achieved.
6. *Standards for evaluation*—"six-point"—The writing is to satisfy all points of the six factors which are listed as vital areas of consideration.

Any learning goal *does* include all six of these factors, and a well-stated learning goal *should* identify them specifically. So that you might be able to do a better job of writing this kind of learning goal, the remainder of the chapter will be used to explain these six factors and to illustrate how they can be used in various adult learning experiences.

The Relevance of the Learning Goal to the Real Needs of Adults

The purpose of educational objectives and learning goals is to change the lives of individuals in some way: their attitudes or value system, their knowledge in a particular area of thought, or the skills which they can use in a given situation. Such educational aims, however, do not spring forth by themselves. The sources of educational purposes are always discovered in the needs of learners.

The learning leader of adults should not blindly accept the learning goals which are given to him in the curriculum materials. Aside from the possibility that they may be stated incompletely or vaguely, there is the chance that such learning goals are not based on the particular needs of those adults in his group. The learning leader needs some basis for determining the real needs of his group. Sources for the discovery of such needs include:

1. What the Bible says about the needs of adults;
2. What adults themselves say about their needs, as determined through surveys, in private or group discussion, or by noting their response to various types of programs or lesson materials;
3. A study of the everyday life of adults;
4. An examination of experts' opinions in the fields of adult education and Christian education (This examination should include reading and studying various books on the subject of adult developmental psychology.);
5. An analysis of the learning leader's own opinion, as he reflects on his own needs and recalls what he knows about the adults whom he leads.

A thorough study of such sources will reveal a multitude of needs. Obviously, not all of these needs can be dealt with in one learning session. The important idea, however, is that *all objectives and learning goals must be based on the real needs of adults in the adult learning group.* Only this concept gives adequate reason for suggesting specific learning goals.

Note that in some cases the real need is present, but the adult learners are unaware of or perhaps in opposition to that need. Such situations call for long-range cultivative planning and preparation. The best learning occurs when the adult is aware of his need and is placed in a position where that need can likely be met. Learning leaders must often be patient in leading adults to become aware of their needs. Only then can maximum teaching results be obtained.

THE IDENTIFICATION OF THE SUBJECT MATTER INVOLVED

In order to secure the greatest effect from learning goals, the subject matter must be specifically identified. It is imperative to know what a lesson is about. Yet this is not always as simple as it may initially seem.

As an illustration of this, consider the following learning goal which is somewhat typical of what might be found in lesson material:

General Statement of Learning Goal

Class members should understand the biblical
viewpoint that spiritual wealth is more
important than material wealth.

An examination of this learning goal reveals *several* subjects:

1. Material wealth in general
2. The biblical text concerning material wealth
3. Spiritual wealth in general
4. The biblical text concerning spiritual wealth
5. Relationship of material and spiritual wealth

The implication is that each of these subjects must be dealt with if the learning goal is to be attained. Only as subject matter is analyzed can it be determined whether or not too much is being attempted for one lesson. The following guideline will help in identifying what is really included in the subject matter:

1. Is the stated subject matter part of a larger category that *must* be considered before the intended learning can be accomplished? If so, that larger subject needs to be included as part of the subject matter for the lesson.
2. Is it possible to subdivide the stated subject matter into important smaller classifications which are necessary parts of the larger idea? If so, these subclassifications should be listed as elements of the subject matter.
3. When there are two or more subjects, is there a relationship between them that must be considered a separate subject matter category? If so, identify that relationship and list it with the other subjects.

THE EXPECTED BEHAVIOR INVOLVED IN THE LEARNING GOAL

It is not enough just to have a subject—something must be done with it. Whatever the learner is to do with that subject matter is called the *behavior*. The learning leader must have definite ideas about what he expects from his learners. Note that the emphasis is not on what the *leader* does but on what the *learner* does. The learning situation is for the learner, not just the teacher or leader. A leader might produce a work of art in presenting program material, but unless the learner has some kind of response, it is doubtful if real learning has occurred.

While it is not always possible to observe evidence that real learning has taken place, it is educationally advantageous to plan learning goals and activities so that at least *some* specific behavioral change by the learner will have occurred, either during the program or at an identifiable future time. As long as the learning leader can know that *some* learning has occurred, he can also be assured of the probability that certain amounts of immeasurable learning have occurred.

As these expected behaviors are stated, however, care must be taken to specify as nearly as possible what is actually intended. Notice the problems that arise when a learning goal is given in vague terminology. The typical, general statement quoted in the previous section was:

> Class members should understand the biblical viewpoint that spiritual wealth is more important than material wealth.

The intended behavior involved in the learning goal is obviously the word "understand." The question is, however, what is really intended by "understand"? This word, and others like it, may mean different things to different people. There is no "meeting of the minds" when curriculum writer, learning leader, and learner all have conflicting ideas about what a learning goal means. The need is for a classification of learner behaviors that makes clear the slight variations in meaning. Bloom's Taxonomies provide a basis for such a distinction of educational behaviors.* The learning leader's choices for selecting possible learning behaviors might include the following:

1. Recall or identification of terminology regarding any subject matter
2. Recall or identification of specific facts
3. Recall or identification of concepts or complex ideas
4. Ability to translate one kind of communication into another
5. Ability to interpret a communication for its simple meaning or significance
6. Ability to extend a set of information or events to its logical result
7. Ability to apply previously acquired knowledge or skills in new situations
8. Ability to analyze a communication for complex and obscure meanings and relationships
9. Ability to produce an original communication
10. Ability to evaluate information or relationships, using specified criteria or standards of judgment

With this classification, it is now possible to analyze the word "understand" and make a decision concerning what is actually intended. Normally, the term "understand" would imply *at least* that the learner be able to interpret the material for its simple meaning or significance. But notice that before a learner can do this, he must be able to translate that material from its given form into his own means of communication. And before this is possible he must know certain concepts, facts, and terminology. All of this is to say that the learning behaviors shown above build on one another. When a high level of learning behavior is se-

---

*Benjamin S. Bloom, *Taxonomy of Educational Objectives, Handbook I: Cognitive Domain* (New York: David McKay Co., Inc., 1956) and David R. Krathwohl, *Taxonomy of Educational Objectives, Handbook II: Affective Domain* (New York: David McKay Co., Inc., 1964).

lected, it may automatically imply a number of other learning goals on a lower level have been reached, when they actually have not. This explains why so much of our "teaching" is never really learned.

The leader's task is to recognize and enumerate all levels of learning behavior for each subject, then determine which of the foundational skills and knowledge his learners can realistically be assumed to have acquired already. In cases where more basic information or skills are required, the learning experience must include provision for this background before high levels of behavioral learning can be successfully attempted.

Notice that in listing the several desired outcomes that are actually involved in a seemingly simple learning goal, it is possible to explain why the results of a program or lesson are often less than expected. Many times a learning leader thinks he is dealing with only one goal, while in reality he is having to fill in the background for several other unspecified or unidentified learning goals. As with the analysis of subject matter, a close look at the full scope of behaviors intended may produce more real objectives than can be handled in one learning experience. If so, then the learning leader has a basis for determining the priority of the learning goals.

THE VALUE WHICH THE LEARNER SHOULD PLACE ON THE LEARNING GOAL

Suppose a Sunday School teacher states his learning goal as follows: "Each class member should be able to recall from memory the Ten Commandments." In all probability, this is not really the only outcome intended. When pressed for an elaboration of what is meant, most teachers would admit that in addition to the mental skill noted above, they also want the learner to *value* the behavior to a certain degree. For example, the teacher may actually intend for this to be his goal: Each class member should be able to recall from memory the Ten Commandments and should accept them as worthwhile moral values. With different learners, the degree of valuation might be more or less.

As was the case with learning behaviors, these possible values need to be summarized in some logical arrangement from which learning leaders can select the specific level which they intend for a particular goal. Again, Bloom's Taxonomies provide a helpful array of educational attitudes illustrating most of the value outcomes dealt with in a given learning situation.

1. Awareness.
2. Willingness to receive
3. Controlled or selected attention
4. Consent to respond
5. Willingness to respond
6. Satisfaction in response
7. Acceptance of a value
8. Preference for a value
9. Commitment to a value
10. Formulation of a value system
11. Characterized by a value system

Notice that in this arrangement of values there is an increase of intensity which is shown in at least two ways:

1. The quality and quantity of attention on the part of the learner increases from a simple awareness to a total mental investment.
2. The learner changes from a passive to an active role. Not only does the subject or idea involved receive more attention by the learner, but in the latter stages of development his actions change because of this valuation.

The leader who is formulating learning goals must recognize that involved in every goal is the element of attitude or value. This factor of value needs to be viewed in two respects:

1. The learner begins the educational experience with a certain attitude or value regarding the subject matter and behavior which is being dealt with.

2. The learner *ends* the educational experience with a particular value.

The learning leader will specify the intended valuation which he desires for the learner to develop. It is unrealistic to set this level much above the beginning level. Solid increases of valuation by a learner are normally in small additions. Many of the newly acquired values must be tested and tried in the learner's mind before the learning becomes permanent.

Note also that both the beginning value held by the learner and the intended ending value set by the leader play important parts in the types of activities and methods which the learning leader will employ to reach his goal. When a group is giving the leader only controlled attention, he will use motivators and activities quite different from instances in which he leads a group that is already committed to a particular value regarding some specific subject.

The Conditions Under Which the Learning Goal Is to Be Verified

All learning will occur under one condition or another. Learning goals need to describe those important conditions which the leader intends to be present when learning is verified. Compare the following statements:

1. Each trainee will be willing and able to select teaching tools that can be used to convey ideas during the following learning situation . . .
2. When provided with a clear, black ink, pica style, typed list of twenty audio and visual aids, each trainee will be willing and able to select teaching tools that can be used to convey ideas during the following learning situation with a class of ten and a room 20 feet by 20 feet containing two electrical outlets and three windows with dark shades. . .
3. When provided with a list of twenty audio and visual aids, each trainee in a class of ten will be willing and able to

select teaching tools that can be used to convey ideas during the following learning situation . . .

It is apparent that the conditions given may include too little or too much description. A sensible level of assumptions must be made, and the description should include only the important conditions which significantly affect the learning situation. The third example is adequate in its description of the conditions.

A clear statement of the intended conditions is really nothing more than what is required for good communication. If the learning leader had a class of three or three hundred in mind instead of ten, then failure to communicate this idea (as in example No. 1) would produce a significant misunderstanding.

THE STANDARDS BY WHICH LEARNING GOALS CAN BE EVALUATED

Every learning goal has standards by which it can be evaluated. In situations where those standards are not stated, they are either clearly implied or unclearly stated. In some ways, both the learner and the learning leader need to know what constitutes performance. While it is not *always* possible to be specific about these criteria or standards, it is important to list what *can* be determined. The formulation of such criteria is improved through practice and through a constant asking of such questions as:

1. What descriptive terms or units of measure can be applied to this activity?
2. What are the worst, average, and best possible responses to this activity?
3. What level of learning am I willing to accept as satisfactory?

The inclusion of standards for evaluation would change the learning goal listed above to read:

When provided with a list of twenty audio and visual aids, each trainee in a class of ten will be willing and able to se-

lect ten of the possible twelve teaching tools that can be
used to convey ideas . . .

A further implication is that inclusion of these standards often
makes it necessary to devise evaluative instruments or situations
in which the measurement can take place. For example, in the
learning goal above, a list of twenty audio visual aids, including
twelve appropriate to the situation described, plus a description
of a learning experience, would have to be devised in order to
test the ability of the learners to achieve the goal. Such evalua-
tions are not easy and most learning leaders neglect them. The
result of this neglect, however, is that learning is indefinite and
usually ineffective. The result in every such case is that learners
and leaders alike didn't know where they were going or whether
they got there! The best way of positive guidance in educational
work is to know the goal and to have a specific way to measure
progress toward that goal.

POSSIBILITIES IN WRITING THE LEARNING GOAL

Criteria for clear statement of learning goals have been listed
above. For a learning leader to include all the needed information in one sentence is possible, but sometimes not feasible. The
important principle is that all criteria be dealt with and noted.
This implies that a simple listing of the factors involved in each
be made. From this listing, the intent of the leader can be
communicated and used for planning purposes. At times, the
statement of a learning goal will need to be followed by a statement such as, "This means specifically that . . . ," and the goal
must be illustrated or further defined.

The writing of clear, concise, helpfully stated learning goals
is a help to learning leaders, not a hindrance. If it is necessary
to do more planning in order to develop these high quality goals,
the cost in time and effort will be repaid by the increased effectiveness of the learning group as it discovers that significant
Christian learning is within reach.

EXAMPLES OF LEARNING GOALS

Sunday School Learning Goal Illustrated

Suppose you are a teacher of Adults in the Sunday School. A typical lesson might be as follows:

TOPIC: *Worship Through Service*

BIBLE PASSAGE: *Matthew 21:28-31a:* But what think ye? A certain man had two sons; and he came to the first, and said, Son, go work to-day in my vineyard. He answered and said, I will not: but afterward he repented, and went. And he came to the second, and said likewise. And he answered and said, I go, sir: and went not. Whether of them twain did the will of his father? They say unto him, The first.

SUGGESTED GENERAL AIM: To guide class members to recognize their need to worship through service in the Lord's work.

Based on your newly acquired insights into the process of goal writing, you recognize that you will have to rewrite the suggested aim. Using the six-point outline developed in this chapter, you might go through the following process:

1. *Need:* My class members need to receive the spiritual blessings that come from serving Christ through worthwhile church work. I know this need is real because the Bible says it is, because many other Christians say so, and also because I know the blessings I have received as a teacher.
2. *Subject Matter:* Christian service.
3. *Expected Behavior:* Application of knowledge by choosing a place of service in a new situation.
4. *Value:* Willingness to respond. This response will be of a free nature with no undue pressure to conform or respond being used. An opportunity will be provided for learner to reject the hoped-for response without embarrassment.
5. *Conditions:* The learner will be presented an opportunity

to choose a place of service in the church immediately or some time in the future.

6. *Standards for Evaluation:* The goal for this lesson will have been attained when one of the following occurs:
   a. Without being forced, the learner volunteers for a place of work in the church.
   b. Without being forced, the learner commences training for a specific place of church leadership.
   c. Without being forced, the learner responds verbally or in writing that he is interested in a specific place of service.

RESTATEMENT OF LEARNING GOAL

When presented with an opportunity for immediate or future Christian service, each class member should be willing to choose at least one area of church work and express written or verbal intent to participate in that activity. This means specifically that each learner must first have knowledge of the facts and concepts involved in the proposed places of service, and then be able to translate, interpret, and extend this information into communication that has personal reference for himself.

Activities that lead to achievement of the learning goal are many and varied. Note that *whatever* activities are selected, they must work in three directions:

1. Changing the attitudes or value system of the learner regarding service;
2. Broadening the learner's knowledge of the subject matter;
3. Giving the learner opportunity to consider mentally the behavior that is going to be expected of him at the conclusion of the lesson.

POSSIBLE ACTIVITIES

1. Begin with an attitude- and interest-changer. (A large sign greets all persons entering a certain manufacturing

plant with these words: "If you are like a wheelbarrow—going no further than you are pushed—you need not apply for work here.")

2. Pass out employment sections of last week's newspaper. Have class members circle ads that substantiate the same idea mentioned in the "wheelbarrow" illustration, such as "no loafers need apply," "this job requires someone who is willing to work," "if you really want to advance."

3. Let class members help in calling to mind a variety of church jobs that need to be filled year after year. Include work that takes practically no special training, as well as work that requires much training. Let the class suggest the priorities of the qualifications involved, with particular reference to the requirements noted in the newspaper ads and the spiritual characteristics of willingness to serve God and dedication to helping others.

4. With the above as a background, conduct a thorough study of the Scripture passage. Include the background for the lesson, an analysis of the responses of each son, and an evaluation of the effect on the father.

5. After closing with illustrations, discussion, or testimony regarding the value of service, hand out Christian Service Survey forms which include opportunities for church work of many kinds. Make sure the form has a separate response for immediate and for future acceptance of a church position or place of work. Give adequate time for the surveys to be completed, then provide opportunity for class members to leave the form with you or to take it with them to complete later. Remain after class for any members who might want to speak to you privately about Christian service.

6. After class members have left, note in your own records the specific areas of interest or decision for each learner, then submit the surveys to the church office. Be sure that there is some kind of follow-up on special decisions.

Church Training Learning Goal Illustrated

The material for a teacher training class refers to the idea that each teacher trainee should "learn how to understand the individual class member." Realizing that "understand" can be interpreted many ways, you list several implications, one of which is the following illustration:

1. *Need:* The prospective teachers need to know what their class members are trying to tell them emotionally.
2. *Subject Matter:* Literal, spoken communication of other persons.
3. *Expected Behavior:* Ability to interpret into emotional content.
4. *Value:* Satisfaction in response.
5. *Conditions:* When listening to other people talk.
6. *Standards for Evaluation:* The goal will be attained when prospective teachers report more than one example of interpretation experienced during the week.

Restatement of Learning Goal

When listening to other people talk, each teacher trainee will derive satisfaction from his ability to interpret the literal, spoken communication into emotional content. This will involve single-mindedness on the part of the teacher trainee, who in listening to the other person will mentally discard meaningless verbal content and persevere in the thought, "What is this person really trying to tell me emotionally?" The degree of satisfaction derived by the learner from this activity will be determined by the number of examples which he reports the following class session. Only one example will be required as outside assignment but more *than one example will indicate a value of "satisfaction in response."*

Possible Activities

This learning goal will involve only two basic factors: insight concerning the skill of emotional interpretation, and practice in applying that skill. Both of these factors can be dealt with in many different ways, but the following should provide results as desired, while at the same time contributing to the achievement of certain other course goals.

1. Structure a class situation where teacher trainees are required to voice their opinions or feelings regarding some subject. This could be a time of testimony or could be an evaluation or analysis of the previous week's work.
2. When completed with the above, introduce the subject of interpreting spoken communication into emotional content. In appropriate cases, use the previous testimonies or verbal expressions as a basis for class discussion on what the emotional content was. For a check, ask the person who did the speaking if the class analysis was accurate. Use as many of these cases as time allows.
3. Just before the training session is over, let the teacher trainees respond to a more formal test of ability such as the following:

> An inexperienced preacher talked to a number of young boys and girls one Sunday morning. After he finished a long string of complex theological terms, one boy turned to another and said, "Where did the preacher get all those big words?" Noting that the minister had used a large, bound book (really a Bible), the second lad replied, "I guess he got 'em out of that dictionary he used in place of the Bible." What do you think the second boy was trying to say emotionally?
>
> ☐ a. The preacher shouldn't read from that dictionary.
> ☐ b. I wish the preacher would read out of the Bible.
> ☐ c. I wish the preacher would talk to us on our level.
> ☐ d. Those long words must have come from that dictionary.

Note those who chose an incorrect response. Discuss the

correct interpretation (c.). If several members missed the test item, give another similar example.

4. Assign each trainee at least one case study during the coming week in which they are to listen to someone's conversation and interpret the emotional content. Have them take notes after the case study so they can share the example with the group the following week.

5. On the following week, determine how many examples each teacher trainee engaged in. One illustration, the required amount, would indicate a level of "willing to respond." More than one example would indicate a degree of "satisfaction in response." Discuss the interpretations of other group members. Repeat the assignment often enough during the entire course that members will continue developing the skill.

4

Choosing Methods
for
Group Learning

THE MAJOR PURPOSE of this chapter is to help you gain skills in understanding when and how to use appropriate methods in adult learning experiences.

Those who seek to lead adults have accepted the responsibility of helping adults with their growth in the Christian life. The group learning experience is one of several powerful influences in the learner's maturation. It is important, therefore, what happens in the group.

Methods and activities of learning make communication within the fellowship of learning possible. Conversation or dialogue with God and each other is the medium through which we are reconciled and become reconcilers. This is the kind of learning environment in which the Holy Spirit leads learners to truth.

Sara Little reminds us that:

> Men need feel no pride in their own accomplishment
> when it is evident that a truly redemptive community
> has come alive. This cannot happen without their full

and free response to God's seeking love, it is true, but it is the Holy Spirit who creates real fellowship—koinonia.[1]

The choice of methods, therefore, cannot be treated lightly. Activities and procedures of learning can mean the difference between a cold, lifeless experience and one which involves the learner, stimulates him toward spiritual growth, and achieves the goals for which learning was planned.

A word of caution is needed. Methods inappropriately used can become ends in themselves. If this be the case, they are little more than gimmicks and devices. No method is of itself effective or ineffective. As Bergevin, Morris, and Smith point out, "procedures are not panaceas. They are not magic pills that guarantee success."

Methods or procedures in learning have little value unless there is something to study. Leaders should avoid the temptation of becoming enamoured with the procedures of learning, to the neglect of the content. On the other hand, intelligent leaders may possess deep insights into the content but cannot share these insights because they lack skills in communication. Developing the ability to use learning methods and procedures sharpens your group communication facility.

There are some basic recognitions upon which the content of this chapter is based. These are:

1. Learning methods or procedure cannot be appropriately chosen until the learning goal or goals have been identified. The learning goal interprets the types of behavior toward which the learner will be led. Once these have been identified, the leader can then ask himself, "How can I devise a learning situation which will produce this kind of behavioral change?"
2. Each learning group is unique. A procedure that works well with one group may not work in another.
3. All in the learning fellowship need to learn how to learn. Some leaders may have once tried new procedures of

instruction and long since given them up, because the learners didn't know how to cooperate. When new procedures are used, learners must be taught how to use them.

4. A variety of methods can be used in a particular learning experience. Several methods may be used together. However, variety never should take precedence over appropriateness.

5. Room arrangement will have much to do with the effective use of methods.

LEARNING GOALS AND METHODS

In the previous two chapters we dealt with the three kinds of learning outcomes or goals that may be desired in a learning situation. Can you recall these? You are correct if you said *cognitive* or *knowledge outcomes, affective* or *attitudinal outcomes,* and *action* or *skill outcomes.* Refer to the examples of these types of aims illustrated in chapter 2.

Remember that learning goals call attention to the types of changes which take place in the learner, not just the teacher. Goals are written for the learner. Therefore, with the goal in mind, you must try to pre-live the learning session. Think about the kinds of learning activities that more likely will help the learner achieve the specified goal.

It is not easy to pre-live the learning experience. The more you practice, the easier it becomes. You must learn to use your best judgment.

In the following paragraphs, an attempt is made to classify certain types of methods and procedures with specific learning goals. These are the twenty-five different methods which are discussed and diagramed in this chapter. Such a classification is, at best, arbitrary.

Many of the methods could be used in achieving all three kinds of learning goals. But a method tends to lend itself more toward certain types of goals than others. The classification given suggests those methods of learning which are more likely to bring about predominant changes when using a specified learning goal.

Cognitive or knowledge outcomes.—When you are seeking to assist the learner with increased understanding or gain in knowledge, consider using:

1. Book report
2. Lecture
3. Panel
4. Question and answer
5. Research and report
6. Symposium

Affective or attitudinal outcomes.—When you are seeking to produce changes in the way a learner feels, consider the use of:

1. Brainstorming
2. Case study
3. Debate
4. Film talk-back
5. Group discussion
6. Inductive Bible study
7. Interview forum
8. Lecture forum
9. Music forum
10. Panel forum
11. Play reading
12. Role playing
13. Seminar
14. Small study groups
15. Symposium forum

Action or skill outcomes.—If the desired changes in the learner require overt behavior or doing something, consider using the following:

1. Demonstration
2. Field trip

3. Work groups
4. Workshops

A combination of outcomes.—It is always best to make your learning goal as specific as possible. In other words, it ought to be either more knowledge-, feeling-, or action-oriented than any of the other two.

In Christian learning experiences, behavioral changes that bring about right action in living should be the chief goal of the leader. Therefore a knowledge outcome may produce a change in feeling or acting. It should be noted, however, that outcomes which emphasize changes in feelings are more likely to produce change in action than those which major only on the accumulation of knowledge.

SIZE OF THE GROUP AND METHODS

One of the best arguments for small classes and groups has to do with the possibilities for learning. Research in the field of education reveals behavior change or learning is more likely to take place in a situation which allows the learner to interact with the leader and other learners.

Have you ever considered the number of relationships which potentially exist in a group? Some definite implications for group size result from such a study. Examine carefully the diagram on page 73.

A study of this diagram would indicate that when three people engage in conversation, there is a pattern of six interpersonal relationships. Add a fourth and the number of relationships increases to twelve. As the number of people increases, the possibilities for interpersonal relationships increase geometrically to produce the following equation: *The number of relationships (r) equals the number of persons in the group (n) multiplied by one less than the number of persons in the group (n-1).* Such a formula is expressed in the equation $r = n\ (n\text{-}1)$. If you are

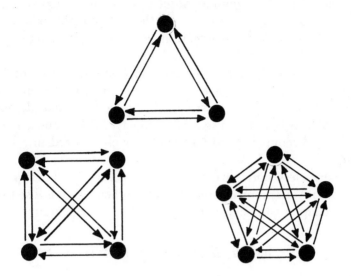

mathematically inclined, try this out on the group of which you are a member.

The implication is that the larger the group, the less possibility of close interpersonal relationships among group members. When a group exceeds fifteen to twenty participants, the number of members who are able to participate would be somewhat limited. The more aggressive learners would tend to dominate and thus diminish the contribution of the less aggressive.

This kind of information would argue in favor of smaller groups as opposed to the very large groups or classes that may still exist in some churches. Do you see how the individual needs of the learner can best be met in a smaller group?

If your group is a Sunday School class, an ideal size would be 15–20 participants, with 25–30 enrolled. In a member training group, the ideal size would be 15, with 20–25 enrolled. In a missionary education group, the number would be best determined by the purpose of the group, with 15 the suggested maximum number. *A word of caution:* Adult groups can be too small. A guiding rule of thumb to follow is: the group ought to be large enough to be organized for learning and yet small enough to allow for learning.

Some groups in our churches are much larger than those just suggested. But the larger the group, the more communication has to become a "one-way street." Some methods, like the case study, field trip, group discussion, inductive Bible study, music forum, and seminar could not be effectively utilized in a large group.

Nevertheless, don't give up on the idea of using other types of methods if your group is large. All of the other methods discussed in this chapter can be used in both small and large groups.

FACILITIES, EQUIPMENT, AND METHODS

A teacher in a Sunday School conference rather apologetically remarked, "The only method of teaching I can use in my class is the lecture method. You see, my class meets in the chapel and it's rather difficult to move the pews." While it is true that methods are limited somewhat by the facilities, many of the methods discussed in this chapter can be used in rooms where seating is considered permanent. The truly creative leader is not inhibited by restrictive facilities. Rather, he is one who is adaptive enough to get the most mileage out of what is available. In the meantime, use your influence with the church council and other planning groups. Encourage them to recommend to the church the procurement of the best facilities and equipment the church can afford.

Two major questions are always asked when the subject of facilities and equipment arises. These are: What size should the classroom be? and What basic equipment is needed?

Suggested room size.—The Adult program leaders and the Church Architecture Department of the Convention recommend, as a minimum, 11 square feet per person in the classroom and 7 square feet per person in the department assembly. However, if you can afford to do so, increase the size of the classrooms. If you use some of the methods described in this chapter you need room! Sacrifice assembly room space, if need be, to protect classroom needs. Twelve to fourteen square feet per person in the classroom would provide adequate room.

Needed equipment.—Budget limitations may restrict the church in what equipment it can provide for Adult classrooms. Basic equipment would include folding chairs (preferably with fold-down writing arm), a small teaching table, chalkboard with picture rail, tack board, maps, learning aid materials, easel, proper lighting and ventilation, and one large folding table for every three to six rooms.

Additional equipment would include a phonograph, access to tape recorder and a video-tape machine, access to an overhead projector, picture collections, adequate church library resources (including audiovisual equipment, Bible atlas and dictionaries, commentaries, biographies, indexes, fiction, filmstrips and slides).

Be alert to new instructional aids and equipment that are being made available. A revolution is taking place in the educational world. These explosive changes are making available to Christian adult education techniques and devices which enhance the learning process.

Excellent supplementary materials are being produced by the agencies and boards of the Convention. Secure these when you order your church literature. These materials include such things as records, tapes, picture sets, maps, posters, flip charts, programed instruction materials, and related books and pamphlets.

Twenty-five Instructional Methods

On the following pages, twenty-five methods are discussed. Each method is illustrated by a diagram. Study these carefully to discover the dynamic factors that are potentially present when learners and leader interact with each other.

You should observe very carefully the "conversation flow" of each method. In some of the more formal methods like the lecture, there is very little verbal exchange between the learners and the leader. Communication is largely *one-way*. In other methods, the arrow illustrates a *two-way* communication between a learner and the leader. When learners are free to address and respond to the leader and other learners, three arrows are used to indicate this conversation flow pattern.

Selected Methods for Cognitive Outcomes

1. BOOK REVIEW

Definition.—An enlisted person studies in advance then summarizes and interprets to learners the concepts of an assigned book.

Goal.—To secure and share information.

Responsibilities of leader.—(1) Enlists someone to study the content of a book; (2) during preparation, raises questions about the content; (3) identifies highlights and points of interest; (4)

makes note of controversial issues or points of disagreement; (5) plans an interesting way to present material to group; (6) uses learning aids or devices to summarize major points.

Responsibilities of learners.—(1) Directed by reviewer to listen purposively; (2) seek to relate content of book to learning goal(s); (3) search for new concepts and seek to incorporate these into thought processes; (4) critically analyze author's point of view; (5) may be asked by leader to discuss and evaluate.

2. LECTURE

Definition.—LeRoy Ford defines it as "the orderly treatment of a particular subject in a speech for purposes of instruction."

Goal.—To secure and share information.

Responsibilities of the lecturer.—(1) Carefully researches the subject; (2) synthesizes pertinent data or information; (3) arranges the material in an organized and meaningful way; (4) plans an interesting and clever way to share information; (5) maintains good eye contact and personal rapport with learners;

(6) uses clear language; (7) summarizes main points with appropriate audiovisual aids; (8) may plan for limited learner participation by combining lecture with other methods or techniques, such as question and answer or listening; (9) helps learners relate information to learning goal; (10) leads the group to evaluate learning.

Responsibilities of learners.—(1) May be directed by leader to read and research in advance the material to be shared; (2) listen purposefully to verbal presentation; (3) seek to relate new ideas to older learnings; (4) take notes on major points of emphasis; (5) participate as directed by lecturer; (6) determine how information may be personally used; (7) share in evaluation of learning.

3. PANEL

Definition.—Three or more resource persons engaged in a purposeful conversation on an assigned subject.

Goal.—To secure and clarify information.

Responsibilities of the leader.—(1) Enlists resource persons based on their competency and interest in the subject; (2) submits questions that may be discussed to panelists; (3) guides panelists in their advance preparation; (4) plans with panelists an agenda of the session; (5) assigns to learners in advance, background study and research problems; (6) arranges for a table and chairs in front of the room for himself and panelists; (7) establishes and states to the group certain "ground rules" and procedures; (8) introduces panelists; (9) states the discussion problem or learning goal; (10) moderates the panel and directs questions to appropriate panelists; (11) encourages panelists to do independent thinking; (12) avoids editorializing on expressed viewpoints of panelists; (13) clarifies and summarizes issues; (14) guides group in thinking about practical application of information; (15) leads the panelists and group in evaluating learning.

Responsibilities of learners.—(1) Complete advance preparation assigned by the leader; (2) listen purposefully; (3) critically analyze various viewpoints of panelists; (4) participate as directed by the leader; (5) if asked, discuss application of information; (6) help evaluate learning.

4. QUESTION AND ANSWER

Definition.—The leader and learners ask questions of each other related to a structured topic.

Goal.—To secure and clarify information.

Responsibilities of the leader.—(1) Assigns to learners, in advance of the session, areas for study and research; (2) prepares a list of related questions; (3) plans to visualize questions; (4) appropriately introduces the subject; (5) directs questions to learners; (6) answers questions asked by learners; (7) summarizes the content of the session; (8) suggests ways to apply information; (9) leads learners to evaluate learning.

Responsibilities of learners.—(1) Complete advance study and research; (2) respond to questions from the leader; (3) direct questions to the leader.

5. RESEARCH AND REPORT

Definition.—The leader presents a problem or issue to the group. Research assignments are made and the group members report their findings at a later meeting (or at the close of the meeting).

Goal.—To secure and share information through research.

Responsibilities of the leader.—(1) Focuses upon research problems; (2) guides the learners in determining the extent to which topic will be researched; (3) calls for volunteers to assume research responsibilities; (4) makes specific assignments to volunteers; (5) secures or directs members to resource materials; (6) guides researchers, as needed, in their work; (7) plans opportunities for researchers to report at the subsequent meeting (or following the session); (8) leads the group in a reaction-discussion following the research reports; (9) summarizes major points of emphasis; (10) evokes discussion of information; (11) guides the group in its evaluation of the learning session.

Responsibilities of the learners.—(1) Support the leader in focusing upon a problem; (2) help the leader determine the extent of the research effort; (3) agree to assume particular research responsibilities; (4) complete specific research assignment; (5) organize the material in a meaningful way; (6) share research findings with the group; (7) challenge presented ideas in order to clarify meaning; (8) suggest possible application of knowledge; (9) aid the leader in the evaluation of learning.

6. SYMPOSIUM

Definition.—Two to five persons give a series of short speeches on different phases of a topic or on closely related topics. (The symposium is different from the panel in that the speakers do not converse with each other. They direct their communication to the audience.)

Goal.—To secure information from the experiences of resourceful persons.

Responsibilities of the leader.—(1) Identifies the problem to be considered; (2) determines the several parts of the problem; (3) assigns background reading to group members; (4) selects resource persons to prepare short speeches on various parts of the topic; (5) prepares with symposium members an agenda for the session; (6) arranges the room to accommodate the method; (7) introduces symposium members to the group; (8) calls attention to the discussion problem; (9) presents in an appropriate way the particular parts to be discussed and the symposium member who is responsible; (10) calls time on the speakers; (11) summarizes the presentations of symposium members; (12) leads the group to think about practical application of knowledge; (13) guides the group in evaluating learning.

Responsibilities of learners.—(1) Complete advance reading or study assignments; (2) listen purposefully to the symposium members; (3) serve, if requested, as a symposium member; (4) think critically about what is said; (5) make notes as suggested; (6) relate new information to old understandings; (7) reflect on new ideas; (8) accept and incorporate into their thinking new concepts or information; (9) help the leader discover ways to apply the concepts and information; (10) share in the evaluation process.

Affective Outcome Methods

1. BRAINSTORMING

Definition.—Brainstorming (idea inventory) may be defined as the spontaneous, "rapid fire" suggestions of a group which represent proposed solutions to a problem. During the period of brainstorming, all ideas are accepted. Evaluation or judgment is withheld until later. (It may be easily combined with other methods.)

Goal.—To secure alternative ideas and proposed solutions to a given problem.

Responsibilities of the leader.—(1) Focuses upon the problem; (2) designates a recorder (or recorders) to write on the chalkboard or newsprint proposed solutions; (3) reminds the group of brainstorming ground rules: keep ideas "popping," state any idea that comes to mind, and resist the temptation to evaluate ideas; (4) stimulates the group for ideas; (5) encourages response; (6) keeps time; (7) stops the group on schedule; (8) leads the group to evaluate suggestions and determine best solutions, or may appoint a committee to study and report; (9) guides the group in determining how the appropriate solutions may be put into effect; (10) evaluates with the group the learning experience.

Responsibilities of the learners.—(1) Think about the solutions; (2) present every possible idea regardless of how ridiculous it may seem; (3) respect the ground rules; (4) participate in the evaluation of ideas; (5) help determine how the information will be put to use; (6) share in the evaluation of the learning experience.

2. CASE STUDY *

Definition.—A detailed, written report describing a real-life situation or problem is analyzed by the group in order to find possible solutions. (It may be easily combined with other methods.)

Goal.—To critically analyze and solve a problem.

Responsibilities of the leader.—(1) Secures a case study or prepares one that is related to a problem; (2) in the writing of a case study objectively considers the following: a. persons involved, b. historical background, c. the relationships and problems which exist among involved persons, religious, social, economic, educational, and ethnic backgrounds of persons involved, d. basic conflicts which seem to cause the problem[2]; (3) lead learners to consider various interpretations of the situations, events, and behavioral patterns related to the problem; (4) guide the group in sizing up the situation; (5) secure from learners tentative solutions; (6) summarize with the group the major

---

* For further study, see *Using the Case Study in Teaching and Training* by LeRoy Ford. (See Bibliography.)

findings; (7) lead the group to determine a course of action for using the information; (8) help the group evaluate the learning session.

Responsibilities of the learners.—(1) Help prepare the case study if requested; (2) read or listen carefully to analyze the case; (3) pinpoint the major issues; (4) discover the role each person plays in the situation; (5) identify behavior patterns that may contribute to the problem; (6) seek to discover why the problem exists; (7) seek to determine what biblical, psychological, sociological, and educational principles might help in the situation; (8) try to discover all possible solutions; (9) focus on the best solution; (10) help evaluate learning.

3. DEBATE FORUM

Definition.—Two speakers who are given equal time present opposing views on a controversial subject. A rebuttal may or may not follow. Following the debate, group members discuss the issues.

Goal.—To obtain opposing views of a controversial issue and get reaction from the group.

Responsibilities of the leader.—(1) Identifies controversial issue; (2) enlists responsible debaters; (3) prepares with debaters an agenda; (4) instructs the debaters to: carefully present point of view, define terms, support view with adequate evidence, attack the opposition, be prepared to defend positions, and provide a summary of the argument; (5) presents the issue to the group; (6) introduces debaters; (7) moderates the debate; (8) leads the open discussion which follows argument summaries; (9) summarizes with the group the main findings; (10) leads the group to think how the information may be applied; (11) guides in the evaluation of the learning process.

Responsibilities of the learners.—(1) Listen purposefully and responsibly to the debate; (2) make notes of statements that may be challenged; (3) share in the group discussion; (4) offer suggestions for follow-through or application of information; (5) participate in the evaluation of learning.

4. FILM TALK-BACK

Definition.—Following the showing, the content of a film, film-strip, or video tape is openly discussed. (It may be combined with several methods like question and answer, small study groups, and others.)

Goal.—To secure information, discover attitudes, and get reaction from group members.

Responsibilities of the leader.—(1) Secures film related to study problems; (2) makes necessary arrangements for equipment, projectionist, and room viewing; (3) prepares and presents a brief introduction to the film; (4) may prepare a list of questions to be answered while viewing; (5) may assign listening teams within the group to listen for specific information; (6) introduces the projectionist and/or shows the film; (7) guides the group in the discussion of related questions; (8) if requested, shows the film again; (9) summarizes group discussion; (10) leads the group to evaluate learning.

Responsibilities of the learners.—(1) Comprehend the purpose of the film; (2) receive the questions to be answered; (3) observe carefully the content of the film; (4) make notes of what is seen and heard; (5) participate in the discussion which follows the showing of the film; (6) cooperate with the leader in deciding on practical applications of the content; (7) help evaluate learning outcomes.

5. GROUP DISCUSSION

Definition.—A topic of mutual interest is purposefully discussed among six to twenty participants under the direction of a competent leader.

Goal.—To develop awareness of other person's feelings, to learn about problems, to enable a participant to express his views, to find solutions to a problem, and to determine a course of action.

Responsibilities of the leader.—(1) Guides the group in determining a topic of interest; (2) assigns background reading to group members; (3) arranges chairs to allow eye-to-eye contact; (4) prepares discussion questions in advance which may be duplicated or visually displayed before the group; (5) cleverly introduces the subject; (6) summarizes the discussion outline to help learners know where the discussion is headed; (7) allows members to modify or add to the discussion questions; (8) opens the floor for discussion; (9) keeps the discussion moving along; (10) stays sensitive to the discussion interests of the group; (11) seeks to draw opinions and conversation from all the group; (12) avoids taking sides; (13) at appropriate intervals, summarizes what has been said; (14) leads the group to apply content of learning; (15) evaluates with the group what was learned.

Responsibilities of the learners.—(1) Complete advance reading assignments; (2) help determine the "agenda" or questions to be discussed; (3) listen purposefully to all that is said; (4) develop sensitivity toward other members of the group; (5) associate meanings with previous learnings; (6) help clarify what is being said; (7) avoid the temptation to monopolize the discussion; (8) accept differences of opinion casually; (9) courteously refrain from engaging in private conversations while a member of the group has the floor; (10) foster understanding rather than force a particular view on others; (11) seek ways to apply knowledge and information; (12) assist the group in evaluation.

6. INDUCTIVE BIBLE STUDY

Definition.—"To induce" means "to lead on" or "to tow." Inductive teaching begins with observations made by learners. Facts and problems are analyzed. Additional facts are searched out. The leader guides the group in narrowing down the research to a statement of principles or generalizations.* Information is discovered by asking such questions as, "What is the biblical writer saying?" "When and where is the writer saying it?" "Why

---

* For further study, see *Straight Talk About Teaching in Today's Church,* Locke E. Bowman, Jr. (See Bibliography.)

is the writer saying it?" "To whom does the writer address his writings?" and "What is God saying to me personally through the words of the writer?"

Goal.—To discover the personal application of what a Bible passage means through a study of Bible resources.

Responsibilities of the leader.—(1) Identifies the lesson passage(s) to be studied; (2) secures necessary study resources, such as translations, commentaries, atlases, dictionaries, and curriculum supplements; (3) arranges the room to accommodate the method; (4) writes on the chalkboard or newsprint the inductive questions stated in the *definition* above (what, where, why, to whom, and so on); (5) may form small study groups or research teams to search particular Bible resources for the purpose of completing specific assignments; (6) serves as a resource person to study groups; (7) moderates the period in which study groups report; (8) summarizes or asks a group member to review the ideas concluded; (9) leads learners to decide personally what the passage means; (10) directs the group in its evaluation of the learning process.

Responsibilities of the learners.—(1) Study in advance the Bible passages; (2) understand the procedures of inductive Bible study; (3) assume responsibilities on small study groups; (4) explore and research resource materials; (5) share research findings with larger group; (6) seek to answer the question, "What is God saying to me personally through this passage?" (7) help the group evaluate learning outcomes.

7. INTERVIEW FORUM

*Definition.—*The leader or designated member systematically questions one or two prepared resource persons on a topic that is of interest to the group.

*Goal.—*To obtain information from authorities and to stimulate the group interest in a topic.

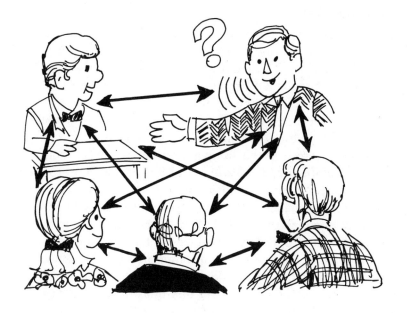

Responsibilities of the leader.—(1) Assigns advance study to learners; (2) focuses on the topic to be discussed; (3) enlists resource person(s) to be interviewed; (4) prepares an agenda which is given to resource person(s); (5) directs the resource person(s) to prepare to answer questions; (6) introduces to the group the topics and resource person(s); (7) directs questions to resource person(s) or introduces designated group-member to do so; (8) moderates questions from the group; (9) reviews the major ideas presented; (10) leads the group to apply learning content; (11) guides the group in the evaluation of learning.

Responsibilities of the learners.—(1) Study materials assigned in advance; (2) critically analyze what resource person(s) say; (3) raise pertinent questions following the interview; (4) synthesize major ideas and concepts presented; (5) assort and assimilate new material into their thinking; (6) think and make decisions about the usefulness of new learning; (7) help the group evaluate the learning situation.

8. LECTURE FORUM

Definition (See *lecture* on page 77.).—A lecture is followed by a free exchange of questions and discussion for the purpose of clarifying issues. (The lecture forum requires more time than the lecture. Excellent learning value is derived from the open discussion that follows the lecture.)

*Goal.—*To secure information from an authority, to enable the group to contribute ideas, and to allow the lecturer to speak to needs and interests of the group as they emerge from discussion.

Responsibilities of the leader.—(1) Enlists a lecturer to speak on the topic of interest (leader may serve as lecturer); (2) suggests resource materials to the lecturer; (3) asks lecturer to carefully organize material; (4) suggests a time limit for the lecture; (5) appropriately introduces lecturer to group; (6) following lecture, moderates the question period; (7) allows lecturer to answer questions addressed to him; (8) allows group members to react to and answer questions from the group; (9) summarizes the main points; (10) guides the group in making

application of the information; (11) leads the group in evaluation.

Responsibilities of the learners.—(1) Complete in advance assigned reading; (2) critically analyze what the lecturer has said; (3) take notes of pertinent ideas; (4) assimilate new information; (5) raise questions following the lecture; (6) engage in group discussion; (7) integrate new ideas in their thinking; (8) decide how learning content may be used; (9) help evaluate the learning process.

9. MUSIC FORUM

Definition.—Choral or instrumental music is heard by the learners, who react to the text, moods, and themes of the music.

Goal.—To respond to, develop appreciation for, and learn from good musical literature.

Responsibilities of the leader.—(1) Secures appropriate musical literature; (2) consults with minister of music for suggestions; (3) arranges for a record player, tape or video-tape

machine; (4) introduces the nature of the music; (5) identifies the things for which to listen; (6) suggests that learners think about such questions as "What purpose did the composer have in mind?" "What moods are created and why?" "What emotions and feelings are evoked by the music?" (7) plays the record or tape; (8) asks for group response; (9) leads group discussion; (10) may replay music or related music; (11) guides the group in summarizing the insights gained from listening; (12) evaluates the group learning experience.

Responsibilities of the learners.—(1) Make preparation for session, such as reading about the composer, studying the musical text, reading about the historical setting that produced the work; (2) learn for what things to listen; (3) discuss with group members reactions to the music, including moods, feelings, and so on; (4) react to other members' reactions; (5) discuss the purpose for which the composer may have written the music; (6) guide the group to think about how the musical content may be applied; (7) help with the group's evaluation of learning.

10. PANEL FORUM

Definition (See *panel,* page 78.).—Following a panel discussion, the group is guided in free and open discussion of a topic.

Goal.—To secure information from authorities and to stimulate participation of the group in the study.

Responsibilities of the leader.—(1) Identifies the problem to be studied; (2) makes assignments to learners; (3) enlists panelists; (4) writes out pointed questions to direct to panelists; (5) plans with panelists on agenda; (6) arranges the room to accommodate the method; (7) presents panelists to group; (8) begins the session with an effective attention-getting device; (9) directs questions to the panel and encourages intra-panel conversation; (10) makes sure that all panelists have a chance to speak; (11) moderates questions from the group and directs the questions to appropriate panelists; (12) clarifies and summarizes major ideas; (13) leads the group to apply knowledge; (14) guides the group in the evaluation of learning.

Responsibilities of the learners.—(1) Complete advance assignments; (2) understand the learning goal and purpose of the session; (3) listen purposefully to the panel; (4) make notes on important ideas; (5) raise questions about controversial or unclear ideas; (6) question panelists following the panel presentation; (7) make decisions about how to apply new information; (8) help evaluate the learning session.

11. PLAY READING TALK-BACK

Definition.—An appropriate play related to the learning problem is read to the group who react to its content.

Goal.—To focus upon a problem, reveal attitudes, and discover solutions.

Responsibilities of the leader.—(1) Select an appropriate play; (2) enlist readers; (3) instruct play readers to rehearse their parts; (4) suggests that they try to identify with the part they read; (5) asks them to be familiar enough with the lines to read them naturally, using voice inflection; (6) arranges the room and play properties; (7) introduces the purpose of the session and the relationship of the play to it; (8) may ask listening teams to listen for specific information, or may distribute a duplicated list of questions for members to answer as play is read; (9) moderates questions from the group; (10) leads in discussion of the questions; (11) if group is larger, may divide the group into small study groups for the discussion of related questions; (12) summarizes discussion; (13) leads the group to make decisions about applying the information; (14) directs the group process of evaluation.

Responsibilities of the learners.—(1) Understand the problem to be discussed; (2) receive questions to be considered while listening to the play; (3) attempt to identify with the characters and problems in the play; (4) participate in the question and discussion period; (5) analyze human relations problems or conflicts revealed in the play; (6) offer possible solutions or alternatives; (7) integrate new ideas; (8) decide how to apply learning; (9) help evaluate the learning session.

12. ROLE PLAYING

Definition.—(A fuller treatment of role playing as a motivational technique is discussed in chapter 5.) Briefly defined, role playing is the spontaneous acting out of a situation by selected members of a group.*

Goal.—To emphasize relationships between people, to evoke self-evaluation, and to discover solutions to a problem.

Responsibilities of the leader.—(1) Focuses upon a problem to be studied; (2) in advance, secures role playing props and arranges the room; (3) explains to the group the life situation to be played; (4) selects or gets volunteers to play the roles; (5) asks

---

*For an excellent study of this method see *Adult Education Procedures: A Handbook of Tested Patterns for Effective Participation,* Paul Bergevin, Dwight Morris, and Robert M. Smith. (See Bibliography.)

role players to leave the room for a brief time to discuss how they will perform; (6) gives introduction of the players to group; (7) cuts off action of the role playing at a climactic moment; (8) de-roles the players; (9) calls for discussion of the situation; (10) leads the group to decide possible solutions; (11) gets an evaluation from role players about their personal reactions to the characters they played; (12) summarizes the major ideas; (13) leads the group in a discussion of application; (14) guides in the evaluation of learning.

Responsibilities of the learners.—(1) Volunteer for parts in the role playing situation (select a role that is opposite from the one played in real life); (2) other members listen and observe the situation; (3) analyze the problem(s) to determine possible solutions; (4) share ideas with other group members; (5) react to the reasons for the behavior in the role play; (6) decide what the situation has to say to their personal lives; (7) help the group evaluate the learning experience.*

---

* See also Leypoldt, pp. 98-99.

13. SEMINAR

Definition.—The seminar is a group of 5 to 30 persons who are directed in study and research by an authority on the subject.

Goal.—To allow members to do depth study, problem solving, and assimilation of data.

Responsibilities of the leader.—(1) Focuses upon the study problem; (2) makes advance research assignments; (3) plans an agenda for the seminar members; (4) introduces seminar members who report on their research projects; (5) moderates the discussion period; (6) summarizes and synthesizes the major concepts revealed in the research; (7) gives a summary speech of the session; (8) guides the seminar members in an evaluation of the learning experience.

Responsibilities of the learners.—(1) Select a research topic based on their interest; (2) complete the research; (3) plan an appropriate way to share the research findings with seminar members; (4) share findings; (5) engage in discussion and evaluation; (6) participate in seminar dialogue; (7) discuss the usefulness of learning; (8) help evaluate the learning session.

14. SMALL STUDY GROUPS (BUZZ GROUPS)

Definition.—Group members are divided into clusters of small groups who meet simultaneously to discuss a problem or complete an assigned task.

Goal.—To permit discussion for all members as an aid in solving problems, identifying needs, and revealing attitudes.

Responsibilities of the leader.—(1) Helps the group focus attention on a problem; (2) divides the group into small groups of three to six per group; (3) states the task for each group; (4) indicates the amount of time allocated for buzzing; (5) asks each group to select a moderator and a recorder; (6) dismisses group to smaller groups; (7) moves from one group to another giving assistance; (8) gives a time warning signal for ending the group study; (9) reassembles the groups; (10) allows time for each study group to report; (11) leads the groups to summarize their findings; (12) guides the group in the evaluation of learning.

Responsibilities of the learners.—(1) Complete assigned study in advance; (2) participate as requested in small groups; (3) offer suggestions and share feelings, opinions, or ideas in the small group; (4) react to other group members; (5) show courtesy to all members of the group; (6) help recorder get down the main ideas; (7) listen to recorder's report to the larger group; (8) add ideas in the larger group discussion; (9) make decisions as to how the information may be used; (10) help with the evaluation of group learning.

15. SYMPOSIUM FORUM

Definition (See *symposium,* page 81.).—Following a symposium, the group participates in free and open discussion.

Goal.—To obtain information from authorities in the field and enable the group to react to the information.

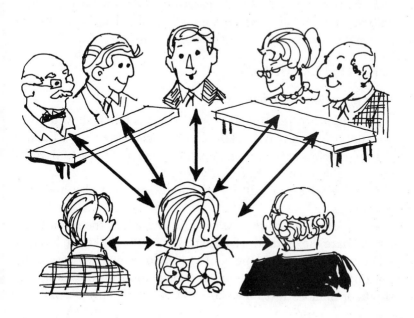

Responsibilities of the leader.—(1) Focuses upon a problem; (2) determines the aspects of the problem to be discussed; (3) enlists resource persons to prepare a short speech on an assigned part; (4) meets with symposium members in advance of the session and prepares an agenda; (5) instructs symposium members to plan a creative way to present the material; (6) indicates the time symposium member will have; (7) assigns study or research to all members in advance; (8) arranges the room to accommodate the method; (9) appropriately introduces the subject in the group; (10) presents symposium members and the part each is to discuss; (11) moderates the discussion period which follows; (12) encourages free and open discussion; (13) leads the learners to apply knowledge; (14) guides in the evaluation of learning.

Responsibilities of the learners.—(1) Complete advance study; (2) understand the nature and procedure of the learning session; (3) make notes as symposium members present their material; (4) assimilate major ideas; (5) relate new learning to old; (6) participate in the discussion; (7) ask for clarification of ambiguous or unclear statements; (8) make decision about the personal relevancy of study material; (9) help evaluate learning.

Action Outcome Methods

1. DEMONSTRATION WORK GROUP

Definition.—A resource person or persons tell or show a group how to perform a certain skill or carry out a procedure. Following the demonstration, members are given a chance to practice or put into action the skill or procedure.

Goal.—To learn a skill by watching someone else and then practicing it.

Responsibilities of the leader.—(1) Arranges the room to accommodate the method; (2) focuses upon the skill to be learned; (3) introduces resource person(s) (leader may serve as resource person); (4) provides detailed explanation of the skill; (5) shows or demonstrates the skill; (6) describes how the skill can

DEMONSTRATION | **WORK GROUPS**

be used; (7) assigns members to small work groups; (8) directs group to practice the skill; (9) suggests that each person have an opportunity to practice; (10) moves from group to group to provide assistance; (11) reassembles the work done in the session; (12) guides the group in the evaluation of learning.

Responsibilities of the learners.—(1) Understand the purpose of the demonstration; (2) carefully observe the demonstrations; (3) think about how they could perform the skill; (4) quiz the resource person(s) to clear up confusion; (5) work in small groups; (6) volunteer to practice the skill in the small groups; (7) learn how to use the skill; (8) help evaluate the learning session.

2. FIELD TRIP

Definition.—A carefully planned trip under the supervision of a well-trained person is made by a group for the purpose of gaining firsthand information.

Goal.—To provide firsthand observation in order to relate theoretical study with a practical application.

INFORMATION

Responsibilities of the leader.—PHASE 1. *Before the trip.* (1) Handles advance arrangements; (2) consults with persons in charge of the facility to be visited; (3) helps orient the group to the place to be visited; (4) outlines the purpose of the trip; (5) arranges transportation for group members.

PHASE 2. *The trip.* (1) Acquaints the group with the guide; (2) supervises the group during the trip.

PHASE 3. *After the trip.* (1) Solicits a report from members on what they saw and heard; (2) summarizes the experiences of the trip; (3) helps the group discover practical application of the experience; (4) guides in the evaluation of learning.

Responsibilities of the learners.—PHASE 1. *Before the trip.* (1) Understand the purpose of the trip; (2) courteously accept the rules and procedures as outlined for the trip; (3) read about the facility to be visited; (4) complete necessary preparations.

Phase 2. *The trip.* (1) Courteously relate to the instructions of the guide; (2) inquire about pertinent facts and items of interest.

Phase 3. *After the trip.* (1) Assimilate data observed; (2) ask questions about what was observed; (3) decide how to use new information; (4) help evaluate learning.

3. WORK GROUPS

Definition.—Assignments are given to designated subgroups for the purpose of accomplishing a task.

Goal.—To develop performance skills through practice and training with others in a group.

Responsibilities of the leader and learners.—For an explanation of how to use this method, study carefully the *demonstration work group* on page 102 and the *small study group* method on page 100. The work group method can be easily combined with several methods. The chief emphasis of this method is to provide time for learners to practice.

4. WORKSHOP

Definition.—Members who identify their interest and needs work out a program of study under the leadership of several authorities in the field. A flexible schedule provides experiences in both general and subgroup sessions.

Goal.—To develop new skills through practice and training opportunities with a group.

Responsibilities of the leader.—(1) Focuses upon the problem to be studied; (2) helps learners discover interests that are related to the problem; (3) enlists appropriate resource persons to provide information for the various interest areas to be studied; (4) provides suggestions and resource materials to resource persons; (5) plans with resource persons a workshop agenda; (6) arranges for facilities and equipment; (7) assigns advance study to the group; (8) prepares a workshop program or booklet which outlines purpose and possibilities of the study; (9) assembles the group for the workshop; (10) helps all group members to become acquainted; (11) presents resource persons and describes resource materials; (12) helps workshop members decide on interest groups they will attend; (13) announces places of meetings for interest groups; (14) makes himself available to all resource persons and workshop members; (15) reconvenes the groups for summary and evaluation.

Responsibilities of the learners.—(1) Understand the purpose of the workshop; (2) complete advance study; (3) choose an area of interest; (4) identify with an interest group or groups; (5) make notes and collect data from groups; (6) learn from the resource person; (7) share in the activities of the work groups; (8) assimilate new knowledge; (9) develop performance skills related to new knowledge; (10) help evaluate the workshop experience.

5

Utilizing
Motivation
Techniques

THE PURPOSE of this chapter is to help you, the leader, understand the significance of motivation as it relates to learning. No learning or change in behavior takes place unmotivated, whether it is learning of facts, skills, or basic values and attitudes.

For that reason, the study of this chapter is significantly important in the understanding of your role and skills as a leader. The chapter will deal with two major concerns of motivation.

First, attention will be given to the matter of getting the adult's initial interest in learning. How to get adults to come to church learning groups has been a constant problem to leaders. For a fuller treatment of this aspect of motivation, you will want to study the new administration books. (For leaders in the Bible teaching program, the book is *Adult Sunday School Work.* For leaders in the church training program, it is *Adults in Church Training.* Adult leaders in missionary education programs should study *Baptist Women Leader Manual, Baptist Young Women Leader Manual,* and *Baptist Men in Missions.*)

The second concern of motivation, which will receive much

fuller treatment, is the matter of getting and maintaining the learner's attention within the group. To help you understand how this may be achieved, insights from motivational and advertising research will be utilized.

The subject of motivation is so complex and inexhaustive that it will be impossible to adequately treat the subject in one chapter. However, what is discussed here should stimulate your own creativity as you learn how to whet the learning appetites of others.

Of course, the Christian Adult leader has access to a source of power that can do more to stimulate a learner than any other one thing. The divine, operative work of the Holy Spirit can do what man cannot do! Before you proceed with the study of this chapter, you might want to read Philippians 2:13. Then study Exodus 4 and notice particularly God's initiative in calling and instructing Moses. Or read Genesis 12:1-4 and learn about God's initiative in calling and instructing Abraham. Isaiah 6 will also help you. Perhaps you might like to review events and experiences of your life which resulted from the dynamic work of the Holy Spirit.

MOTIVATION DEFINED

"No person, no needs. No needs, no motivation. No motivation no education." These phrases by John Fry point up the significance of understanding the learner in such a way that he can be motivated to learn. The problem of motivation is the question of *why*? Why does a person think as he does? Why does he behave as he does? The apostle Paul apparently struggled with this question. Romans 7 gives a lengthy treatment of the apostle's struggle with this kind of question.

Motivation is an essential element of learning. Anything that prompts us to activity or influences us to do something is a factor in the motivation process. Many definitions of motivation have been set forth.

Mehran Thomson summarizes these as follows:

> Motivation is the superhighway to learning. "The organism must be motivated to learn" (McConnell); "Learning will proceed best if motivated" (Anderson); "Motivation is an essential condition of learning" (Melton); "The problem of motivation is central both to educational psychology and to the classroom procedure" (Harris); . . . "Motivation is indispensable to learning. It represents thee antecedent, dynamic background for both original behavior and its modifications" (Gates); "Motivation is the central factor in the efficient management of the process of learning. Some type of motivation must be present in all learning" (Kelley).[1]

What does motivation mean? From the foregoing, we might conclude that *motivation is the process of activating, directing, and maintaining interest in activities which lead to the achievement of a goal.*

Notice that motivation is primarily an *internal process.* Those things which reside within the individual are the important factors that cause him to seek a particular goal. External forces stimulate his interest, but the goals and motives of the learner are his own. It is a proven fact that most learners are indifferent or lazy toward someone else's learning goals. We tend to commit our energies toward goals which we ourselves have come to find desirable.

Adult learning situations in the church, therefore, must be created in which the learner is able to identify for himself worthy goals and motives. As McKinley notes:

> One of the major jobs of an effective adult educator is that of creating opportunities in which people can activate educational goals and motives. This is often called the first step in educational motivation.[2]

MOTIVATING THE LEARNER'S INITIAL INTEREST

Harry L. Miller has suggested that motives in adult education work at two distinct levels. Since most adult educational undertakings are largely voluntary, adults must be motivated to come or to participate. Motives on this level may include intellectual curiosity, the need for human relationship, and status recognition and rationality, the latter referring to the desire to "talk things over."

As Miller notes:

> Motives which are strong enough to bring an individual into the learning situation may be too weak by far to keep him in it for very long or to keep him at work; the very high drop-out rate in adult programs which are not vocationally based is in part a measure of that motivation strength.[3]

But motivation must also be effective on another level, for adults will need motivation to change appropriate behavior. It is at this point that the educator faces the greatest resistance to change, and needs the most help. The major portion of this chapter is related to this type of motivation. However, think for a moment about motivation for participation.

Announcements from the pulpit or in church bulletins, visual posters, and other types of publicity are several ways to stimulate interest. But other types of attention-getting devices may be needed to get adults to a learning program.

"Y'all come" is a frequently heard expression in our churches. "But why?" is an oft unspoken response that the adult voices in answer to this appeal. If he can recognize a personal problem that might be solved by attendance in the program, he is more likely to respond. If he can recognize a personal need or shortcoming that could be met through his involvement, he might more readily identify with the program.

In addition, his anticipation of achieving personally rewarding outcomes within a reasonable period of time evokes the adult learner's attention. When making an appeal to the learner based on the content of study, it is always wise to help the learner understand what he may expect and when. For example, your appeal might say, "After a six weeks' study you will be able to tell and explain what Baptists believe about the doctrines of God, man, sin, salvation, santification, and the church." Or, "After five training sessions you may expect to have the basic skills necessary to work with a group of economically underprivileged in our community."

You may also get the learner's initial attention by helping him recognize that other learners have similar problems. The pathway toward personal involvement in learning is easier if we discover that others of similar need are walking along with us.

If the learner is already a part of the group, you may "latch on" to his interest by allowing him to help you, the leader, determine the kinds of learning activities that will be planned. If he knows that the teacher in the Bible class is anticipating his own needs in the preparation of learning activities, he commits himself to those activities. If he is included in the planning and is asked to participate in the procedures, he will be more intellectually, emotionally, and spiritually involved. If in a church member training group the learner has a voice in what will be studied, he will be more interested in the program. Or if he can choose the mission study, prayer, or action groups that interests him, he is more likely to make productive contributions.

Finally, you may get the learner's initial interest by letting him read, on his own, the content material which the group will study. You may suggest that he read a book related to the study. A programed instruction booklet might let him do an armchair study of the content. Interest aroused in individual study might evoke interest in group study.

You will want to secure sufficient literature and curriculum resources to give to prospective group members, as well as members. An examination of what is being studied by church groups is a good way to motivate adults toward personal involvement. If some adults complain that the church literature is too elementary, give them copies to examine. Such improvement has been made in recent years that this excuse is no longer valid for most people.

Giving a noninvolved adult learner copies of curriculum materials may represent the best investment your church could make for him, especially if instructions and study guides are personally supplied. It would be far better to have him come to the group meeting. But second best might be getting the learner to engage in individual study at his own pace. He may become so interested that he wants to identify with the group. Again, the Holy Spirit, working through inspired writings, can do wondrous things.

Motivation Factors in the Group Learning Process

Having seen the more general nature of motivation, we turn our attention to the application of motivational principles to the teaching-learning situation. What are some factors in the group learning process?

The Leader.—Motivation in the learning process is not only a pupil but also a leader concern. The leader's knowledge of pupils will directly influence the level of motivation. As one noted educator has said:

> To provide motivation the teacher must study and know
> . . . pupils and the groups as such . . . . Ease of moti-
> vation . . . is directly related to his knowledge of the
> learner's characteristics, and to his ingenuity in making
> connection between them and the desired learning ex-
> periences.[4]

Another means of strengthening the will to learn in the learner is for the leader to aid in clarifying goals.

The leader has a special function in capitalizing on motivation which already exists. Jesus, in his teaching, always seized upon the learner's immediate interest. Do you remember how he did this when talking with the woman at Jacob's well? The leader's personal enthusiasm in behalf of the learner's interest is always a good starting place.

As Skinner remarks:

> The only thing that will bridge the gap is interest and
> enthusiasm. Interest may exist to some extent on the
> part of the pupil; more likely it needs to be artfully

created by the teacher. Capitalizing on natural interests and cultivating new ones is the mark of a good educational program.[5]

The curriculum.—Since adults are more inclined to relate learning to immediate needs, curriculum materials must be carefully explained. In some churches, about all that we do is pitch a quarterly to the learner and tell him to go learn.

If, however, the leader can introduce the content of the quarterly, call attention to life needs that are met in the units of study, show the learner how to use the material, and make available additional resources, it will make a difference in the learner's interest.

The group.—The learning group may refer to the smaller, organized unit, or it may refer to the entire fellowship of the church. That the social group is an effective agent in motivation has been shown by several investigators. Havighurst and Orr pointed out that the expectations and values of our society determine the things a person does.

This fact is particularly relevant for the church fellowship. Individuals identified with the church society are molded by what is expected of them. A graduate student at Southwestern Baptist Theological Seminary recently studied the growth patterns of some of the fastest growing churches in America. These churches were scattered throughout the nation and affiliated with several denominations. One conclusion from this study was that the methods utilized were numerous and varied and no one method in itself could be credited with the success. The common factor in all the churches had to do with the motivations of the people resulting from certain expectations for its members inherent in what the church determined its mission and purpose to be. The conclusion is that persons in a society, like the fellowship of a church, will become, in part, what that society expects them to be. If the church expects only half-hearted support from its members, then that's what it gets.

This principle can also be applied to the small learning group. To think of learning merely as an individual process is to overlook the influence of others in the group. The mere presence of others will affect our behavior in learning. There will be group goals as well as individual goals, and the motive of the individual often stems from his identification with the group.

It is, therefore, very urgent that the group seek to pattern itself after the biblical koinonia. Such a fellowship is open and honest, with each person seeking to know and do the will of the Father. It is a spiritual democracy where each member is permissively regarded for his own value as an individual. It is a helping group that seeks to minister to the total needs of individuals. It is a faithful witness to the revealed word from God. This kind of group will provide incentive, encouragement, and excitement for its learners.

The learner.—The fourth and chief factor is the learner himself. All the previously mentioned factors directly affect him. Consider the following motivational realities that are closely related to the learner:

1. Recognize the necessity of the desire to learn; it is essential to effective learning.
2. Motivation will also be generated as the learner becomes conscious of the need for learning. Our earlier discussion of needs emphasized that "behavior is modified only in response to needs." David Ernsberger goes a step further in stating that, not only must needs be present, they must be consciously recognized as such.
3. As previously discussed, the learner needs to know what he is learning and why. His motivations for learning are dependent on this knowledge. The will to learn, or self-motivation, can be achieved by knowledge of results, high aspirations, and clear goals.
4. Remove or overcome negative motives. These negative motives may arise when the learner is not involved and does not see the learning task as personally important, when the learner's objectives have little to do with the leader's, and when the learner is threatened by changes.

These negative motives may be overcome in several ways. For example, make the materials as practical as possible, use "advance organizers" (let the learner see where he is going), organize activities so that the learner will derive satisfactions from new learning before having to relinquish older ideas.

5. Help learners overcome resistance to change. Although there is a need for new experiences in the Christian life, fundamentally, we all tend to resist change. In chapter 1 it was stated that repentance is a prerequisite to change.

To help the learner overcome this resistance to change, consider the suggestions offered by McKinley:

> Opportunities to express our differences.
> Recognition by learners that resistance is natural.
> Willingness to help each other struggle internally with our learning problems.
> Mutual trust among colearners, which frees us from defending ourself as we now are.[6]

6. Assist the learner in overcoming fear. Learning situations bring us face to face with the unknown. Jesus always put his learners at ease by dealing with the unfamiliar in familiar terms. Twentieth-century church leaders can do the same by helping group members really know each other, and by helping the group to realize that the leader wants to be recognized as a learner too.

7. Understand that basic to all motivation is a personal faith in Jesus Christ.

MOTIVATION RESEARCH AND ADULT MOTIVES

The next section of material, at first sight, may seem strange to you. Withhold your judgment about the validity of the approach, however, until you have worked through the rest of the chapter. The last part of this chapter contains some practical material.

Those of us who teach or lead adults in church learning groups can learn from men with experience in the advertising world. Millions of dollars are spent each year seeking to find ways to attract the attention of the buyer. Our understanding of some of these techniques will help us in our effort to stimulate the learning interests of adults.

What Is Motivation Research?

Motivation research is a tool designed to help the manufacturer marketing field. It is a tool designed to help the manufacturer or advertiser to sell more goods. Its aim is to *expose* the market situation, to *explain* it, and in consequence to *suggest* courses of action which will lead to desired changes. Motivation research is among the newest area in marketing research, for it has been employed to a significant extent only since the 1950's.

Motivation research is concerned with the question of *why* people behave as they do. This is a description which is shared by many social sciences, and it is from these sciences, particularly psychology and sociology, that motivation research draws many of its methods and techniques. In fact, Stewart Britt points out that the phrase "motivation research" is a misnomer. It is really an "umbrella term" coined to cover the techniques (called projective techniques) which have been adapted for consumer research and will be described in following pages. However, projective techniques were first used by psychologists to learn something about people's unconscious motives, wishes, desires, aspirations, doubts, and fears. They have very practical use in marketing and advertising, for both of these fields strive to get deeper insight into why people behave as they do and how they could be persuaded to behave differently, in order to plan campaigns with more precision and success.

In search for *why* answers about human behavior, motivation research seeks to relate behavior to underlying processes such as desires and emotions. It recognizes that some people are changeable, suggestible, nonrational, and motivated by emotion, habit, and unconscious causes more than by reason and logic. Each person's behavior is shaped by the ideals and pressures of his society as well.

The aim of motivation research is to cut through the superficial aspects of conduct by the use of projective techniques in order to get a clearer idea of the real person behind the masks.

Actually, from the standpoint of marketing and advertising, however, motivation research is concerned not so much with any one individual's peculiar motives as with motives which are common to broad groups of people. Motivation research then involves thinking in terms of groups of people.

TECHNIQUES USED IN MOTIVATION RESEARCH

In order to get at these variables and thus at the *why* of behavior, techniques devised by scientists of clinical psychology and other sciences are used. As indicated, earlier motivation research can only be defined in terms of the techniques it uses. These borrowed techniques are called "projective techniques." To these we add the interview method. For the purposes of motivation research, they are used to *penetrate below the surface*. That is to say, motivation research is concerned only with getting sufficiently below the surface to do the job of stimulating buying. There is an aim to "plumb right down to the depths of the human soul!" To a very large extent, these techniques are indirect approaches which encourage a person to disclose information about his needs, motives, and so on. They are called *projective* techniques, in the sense that a person projects himself and his feelings and desires into his interpretation of the special materials presented to him.

1. *The depth interview.*—The depth interview is one approach in which the respondent is allowed to talk freely on or around a particular subject. It is carried on without the restrictive use of a questionnaire and with a minimum of interference from the interviewer. The interviewer is responsible for seeing that certain key points are covered in the process of the discussion. To this

end, he is furnished not with a questionnaire but with what is called an "interview guide," which is a list of points to be covered. Skill, training, and experience on the part of the interviewer are necessary. Such an interview may take from fifteen minutes to two hours. This time depends on a number of factors, such as the respondent, his knowledge of and interest in the subject, and the area the interview guide is designed to cover.

Despite its name, the depth interview cannot really go very *deep*. Often the respondent is not aware of what his attitudes really are or what underlying emotions created them, so he can hardly explain them, even in a long interview.

The same approach used in the depth interview can be used for group interviews. For the group interview, a number of respondents are gathered together (4 to 8) and "set" to talking on a given subject. As in a depth interview, the interviewer chairman steers the conversation to cover the point of an interview guide. Notes are taken or the entire procedure is recorded. There are again some recognized disadvantages—it is difficult to get a representative group together in this way, and the conversation may well be dominated by one or two persons. However, it does provide for a number of responses to be expressed, and in such a group, one respondent may trigger a comment from other participants, resulting in a variety and depth of responses.

2. *Projective techniques.*—Projective techniques are indirect methods aimed at persuading the respondent to reveal some aspects of his personality or his attitudes toward a given product or idea as he interprets specially prepared materials. By projecting himself into given situations, he may reveal aspects of his behavior which he would be unwilling or unable to verbalize if approached directly. This unwillingness may be due to a number of factors, one of which is ego-involvement.

Some of the projective techniques are relatively simple to interpret, while others required skilled and sensitive interpreters. There are a number of useful and reliable projective techniques:

(1) COMPLETION TECHNIQUES

a. *Sentence-completion tests.* The respondent is given the

first part or the opening phrases of a number of sentences and asked to finish each of them as he wishes. The "given" phrases have been carefully constructed to avoid giving any clue as to what might be the "expected" answer. The sentences are usually in the first person, but sometimes a third-person format is used. The sentence-completion may be concerned with attitudes toward a particular product or problem, or it may be concerned with the personality of the respondent. One disadvantage is that it does not always manage to conceal just what is the "expected."

b. *Picture-frustration or the adapted forms of cartoon or balloon test.* The subject is provided with a rough sketch or cartoon showing two persons talking in an appropriate setting. The setting is the key. One of the figures has just said something represented by the words written in the "speech balloon" as in a comic strip; the other figure's balloon is empty and the respondent is asked to fill in the empty speech balloon. This test is devised to cover certain aspects of personality. The pictures "break the ice" for talking about a topic.

(2) ASSOCIATION TECHNIQUES

a. *Word association test.* Here the stimulus given is a word, and the respondent is asked to reply immediately with the first word that comes into his mind. Each word in a series is given rapidly so that the respondent is under some pressure and in such a state replies with a meaningful but spontaneous answer. A small number of the words used are key words while the others serve as fillers. This test is thus able to probe into underlying attitudes. Usually this technique is supplemented by one or more of the other projective tests.

b. *Picture probes.* A picture or series of photographs are given the respondent, who is asked to look at them and tell what image occurs to him.

c. *Rorschach Ink Blot Test.* The subject is given a picture as a stimulus and asked to read into it what he sees or perceives. The subject is asked to do this with each of ten cards. Clues to the subject's personality include his reactions to the pictures as well as what he says. This test is very flexible and can be used in depicting the personality of groups or individuals. Thus, it is potentially useful in advertising and marketing.

(3) CONSTRUCTIVE TECHNIQUES

a. Thematic Apperception Test (TAT). This is a specific standardized psychological test used for clinical diagnosis of personality deviations, and it is used with various modifications in motivation research.

The principle of the TAT technique is to show the subject a picture, a drawing, or a series of pictures from magazines, paintings, or drawings. The subject is asked to express freely and in detail what the pictures mean to him. In responding to the picture, the subject is asked to make up a story concerning each picture, telling what the situation is, what the events were that led up to it, and what the outcome will be, describing the feeling and thoughts of the characters. The theory is that in doing this, the person reveals something about himself. An evaluation of the stories is then made which gives the researchers greater understanding of the thoughts and emotions of the person involved. A person's perception depends on his background, experiences, aspirations and desires. TAT can be constructed to measure reactions to an institution, symbol, product, a situation, and so on.

b. Blacky Picture Test. This test consists of a set of 12 cards containing cartoon drawings showing the adventures of a dog named Blacky. They are designed to depict either a stage of psychosexual development or a type of object relationship within that development. Examples are: love object, guilt feelings, and hostility. The pictures are geared to elicit fairly specific types of information.

c. Four Picture Test. Four pictures are selected to portray human situations. The respondent is shown the four pictures with the following instructions: "Here you have four unrelated pictures. Try to build a story that combines these four pictures and brings them into relation with one another." (This test is similar to TAT.) The object is to discover the respondent's general attitude toward life as far as it is determined by his personality.

(4) CHOICE OF ORDERING TECHNIQUES

Here the respondent chooses from a number of alternatives the item or arrangement that fits some specified criterion, such as correctness, relevance, attractiveness. The responses are all given and the subject selects the one or ones that seem most appropriate. These techniques are designed to measure the intensity of attitudes, and the results are illuminating since it can get past the barriers of inarticulation and ordinary verbal response.

    a. Szondi Test

    b. Picture-arrangement test

(5) EXPRESSIVE TECHNIQUES

This group of techniques requires the respondent to combine or incorporate given stimuli into some kind of a novel production. In so doing, the respondent expresses himself in a manner which influences his personal adjustment in light of the situation. The following techniques are examples:

> Play techniques—living newspaper, impromptu theatre
> Drawing and painting techniques
> Writing essays
> Role playing
> Psychodrama

Role playing and psychodrama are closely related. Role playing is a general term referring to the spontaneous acting out of roles in the context of human relations situations. Both require not only players but an audience who helps the players interpret their roles. Role playing deals with the interaction of people with other individuals or groups as carriers of some specified cultural role, such as employee, leader, mother or father, and is used in a group setting. The psychodrama may also be used in a group setting, but it is mainly concerned with the unique problems of a particular individual. So the emphasis in the psychodrama is on the private world of some individual, while in the role play the emphasis is on what is common in the social roles of many individuals. Also, psychodrama needs the guidance of a trained therapist, since it is dealing with an individual's needs and problems.

The above descriptions provide a survey of the techniques used in motivation research. They are often used in combination with one another. It is well to point out that this is one part of marketing research. It is a tool, a powerful one—but it is not a magic wand, nor a new religion, nor a brain-washing technique. Motivation research should not be expected to solve all problems, but it does have an important role to play in attempting to answer the questions of *why*?

APPLICATION OF MOTIVATION RESEARCH
TO CHRISTIAN ADULT LEARNING

The nature of adult learning.—At the outset, it is worthwhile to restate some facts regarding adult learning and the nature of the adult learner. You will recall that an elaborate discussion of this topic was included as a part of the first chapter.

Adult learning is possible, but it needs to be based on the understanding that adults learn best when actively involved, when they recognize a personal reason for learning, and when they share in the responsibility of the learning experience. In addition, it is of value to review the fact that adults are unique, ego-centered, often insecure, fearful, and threatened when faced with the unknown. They have conflicting needs of dependence and independence; they are emotional and resist change. The adult learner is influenced by such variables as needs, motives, self-perception, predispositions, and other external stimuli.

The implication is that adult learning experiences need to be problem-centered and experience-centered, with goal planning shared by learners themselves.

Facing the task.—It is also important that we review some assumptions we often make in facing the task of planning adult Christian learning.

1. We have assumed that all adults want to learn.
2. We have assumed that we have a "captive audience" who is ready to learn.
3. We have been in danger of making Bible knowledge an end in itself, thus separating knowledge from experience.
4. We have perhaps unknowingly assumed that all teaching-learning in the church is positive because of its nature.
5. We have in the past assumed that almost anyone could teach.

PRACTICAL APPLICATION AND EXAMPLES OF VARIOUS MOTIVATION RESEARCH TECHNIQUES

Christian educators can and have learned from the market researcher, and have adapted "projective techniques" with some exciting results in class study, group learning, committee work, and other areas. As in motivation research, the use of these techniques is to "get below the surface" in order to stimulate learning through active participation. These techniques can "break the ice," remove anxiety or masks, reveal needs and concerns of participants, and expose feelings and deep emotions by using an indirect approach. The possibilities are numerous for teaching-learning as the learners project themselves into the interpretation of materials. Several things need to be noted regarding the use of projective techniques:

1. They won't solve all problems in the teaching-learning situation.
2. They can be overused; they should not be misused.
3. They must be chosen carefully and used purposefully.
4. They require time to use.
5. They are not ends in themselves—only means to involvement and to getting at the question of *why*?

There are several examples of many of these techniques. The following are only a few.

1. COMPLETION TECHNIQUE

Sentence-completion tests can be used in a variety of situations. It is difficult to conceal what is the "expected" answer when wording the sentences.

2. ASSOCIATION TECHNIQUES

a. *Word association test.* Suppose a group of adults (parents, youth advisers, leaders) are meeting to discuss the young adolescent. You could use this technique to get at an understanding of the feelings of the young teen-ager. Explain that a series of words will be read one at a time, and each person is to write down whatever word or phrase comes to mind upon hearing the word. Use the following words: *gang, authority, afraid, date, loneliness, parent, church, sex, hate, war, fail, God, dirty,* and *enemy.* This series of words can be used a second time in this way: "What word or phrase do you think a young adolescent would give in response to these words?" Then repeat the list. Finally, the list could be repeated the third time with participants asked to respond with what they would have written when *they* were young teens. Move from this exercise into small groups to discuss the responses. Finally, the total group could reconvene to discuss some of the barriers to communication between the generations.

b. *Picture probes.* Display a series of pictures depicting "displaced persons" (school dropout, rejected or lost child, a victim of war, old person). Ask each class member to tell what image occurs to him. This might be used to get into a study of Isaiah (chapters 40-66).

3. CONSTRUCTIVE TECHNIQUES

Use of pictures. Build a story around the pictures. Do you see how this technique lends itself to motivating the learner's interest? What is the meaning of stewardship? Who is our neighbor and what does he have to do with stewardship? Example 3 could be used in a discussion on sin and judgment. What kinds of sin are shown here? In what way does each suggest the judgment upon us which sin brings? How is the Christian to respond to God's judgment of these kinds?

4. CHOICE OF ORDERING TECHNIQUE

Give this list of words and ask the group to classify or arrange them:

groups	John
Samaria	love
Saul	alms
Peter	disciple
miracle	Pharisee
mercy	temple
apostle	justification
inn	Jericho
lawyer	persecution
lame man	priest
Jerusalem	conversion
Damascus	Levite

The point here is to see that one's frame of reference (revealed in the game) has a bearing on thought processes. Every student brings to the interpretation of the Scriptures a frame of reference that is part of himself. It is into this frame of reference that he seeks to fit what he reads in the Bible.

5. EXPRESSIVE TECHNIQUES

As indicated previously, this is a group of techniques requiring the respondents to get involved in a "novel production." Here is where creativity can be unleashed with exciting insults, insight, and real learning. As in the use of the projective techniques, it takes time to be creative.

a. *Art techniques*—drawing, montage, collage, and so on.

(1) Pipe-cleaner figures allow the expression of feelings and attitudes to occur much more freely than simple discussion. Controversial opinions can get out into the open without threatening the participants. Give each person three pipe cleaners and demonstrate the instructions. For example, you might encourage the participants to make their figures express the adult's view of today's youth.

(2) The montage may be used in many different ways.

Suppose the theme of the discussion is entitled "What's Pressuring You?" Magazines are brought to the classroom. Learners are asked to cut out pictures and paste up a montage which reflects what's pressuring them. Following the creation of the montage, learners could comment on their creations.

b. *Play techniques*

(1) Monologue—A simple form of drama in which one person speaks alone and, for the moment, shares the thoughts and feelings of the character being portrayed.

EXAMPLE 1. What should happen if Zacchaeus came in and told his story? He appears and begins to speak.

EXAMPLE 2. Begin the class session on "The Servant Idea" by shining each person's shoes as they enter the classroom.

EXAMPLE 3. The displaced person (Isa. 40) speaks:

> Do you know how it feels to be what they call a "displaced person," an outsider in the land? No, you couldn't possibly know. You have a home, and a job. You are secure. Your name doesn't have a foreign sound to it. You don't speak with an accent. Your skin is the right color. You own real estate that your fathers owned before you. You have a place in the life of this country. We are different. We are outsiders. We don't belong in these surroundings. Everyone needs to belong somewhere, and we are no different in that respect. It is true that I have never lived anywhere but right here, but that does not make this home. I have a home I've never seen. It isn't a big land, and the scenery is nothing to speak of. But it belonged to my grandfather and his people . . .

This sort of brief drama can open up discussion of such topics as relationships, circumstances, and meaning of faith.

(2) Situation drama—This is an informal drama presenting a social situation in which actors act up to the point of conflict and stop. The discussion picks up on possible ways of handling the conflict. By play-acting a problem as if it were our own, we are able to discuss it more freely and less defensively than otherwise. The parable of the prodigal son (conflicts between parents and teen-agers) could be used effectively.

(3) Informal dramas—Act out the meaning of the empty tomb (John 20:1-18), the meaning of the resurrection, or possibly the Passover feast.

(4) Living newspaper—An illustration of this technique might be to divide the class into small groups. Following the reading of the parable of the prodigal son, each group would be instructed to compose a newspaper account of the event.

(5) Role playing—Role playing is the spontaneous and impromtu acting out of a problem situation. The term "role" refers to the behavior patterns which people learn and live by in our culture. Leaders find role playing valuable for analyzing and solving various problems in human relationships. Through this technique, people can more easily understand their own feelings and comprehend the emotions and viewpoints of others. Consider the following illustration of the use of role playing:

Six persons are involved in role playing a group of adults gathered for a committee meeting. Each of the six participants is given a slip of paper with one of the following roles assigned:

—Seek to guide the group in the right direction, perhaps to the point of dominating it aggressively.
—Seek to relieve tension in the group by humor, perhaps even being a "playboy."
—Compare and try to harmonize all differences, perhaps even to the point of dishonesty.
—Give information, perhaps to the point of talking too much.
—Concentrate on the task of "gate-keeping," perhaps even to the point of failing to give ideas of your own.
—Concentrate on setting standards and keeping the group on the track, even perhaps to the point of some rudeness.

The audience is assigned to observe one of the six participants. After an adequate time, stop the role play and have a coaching session between the participants and the audience observers. The coaches are to suggest to the participant ways he might serve the group better. Then resume the role play. Follow this with a discussion of the role play, with the participants reading their assigned role and then the suggestions received from their coach.

It is important from the beginning to let it be known that the participants are assuming a role and are not being themselves. It is equally important that the participants be de-roled. Sometimes when a person has really thrown himself into a role, it is hard for him to get out of it.

(6) Creative writing—Learning can come alive through various forms of creative expression. Writing is one of these. Learners might develop creative essays on various topics. For example, a housewife in a Kentucky church wrote a moving essay on "If I Only Had Twenty Four Hours to Live." This assignment was made by a study leader in her church training group. Read it and let the creativeness of it benefit your life.

IF I HAD TWENTY-FOUR HOURS TO LIVE

Shirley Bell

If I had only twenty-four hours to live, I'd begin my day at 1:00 in the morning. Being a woman, I'd want my house neat and clean; so, I'd put it in order quickly. I'd try to have everything in its place so that Ed and Vickie and Valerie could find what they needed without my help. You know how it is: "Mother, where are my socks?" and, "Honey, what have you done with my hunting jacket?"

I'd also want to provide something good for my family to eat. So, I'd bake a ham, perhaps, and fix the peach cobbler Ed's so crazy about. These preparations wouldn't take very long, for I'd hurry. Every moment is precious, you know.

Then, I'd put on a warm robe and go outside and curl up in a chair to watch the sunrise for the last time. I'd marvel at the beauty of the mist that always gathers in the hollow across the road, I'd hear the sleepy twittering of a waking bird, and I'd catch a glimpse of a fading star.

Soon the eastern sky would become a kaleidoscope of color, and the rising sun would drench the countryside in golden splendor and transform the dew upon the grass to glittering diamond drops. And I would find peace and joy in the magnificence of God's handiwork.

But time would be passing; so, I'd slip back into the quiet house and put the coffee on to "perk," the ham and eggs in the skillet, and the toast in the oven. Then I'd wake Ed. We'd eat breakfast as usual; and, before we had finished, Vickie would appear, tousle-headed and drowsy; and Valerie would tumble in, too, all warm and rosy from sleep.

Soon we'd pack a little lunch and go for a picnic in our own special place where years of falling leaves have carpeted the ground so thickly that it feels as if we are walking on a sponge.

While the girls gathered flowers and chased butterflies, I'd thank God for making them strong, for making them able to run and sing, and for giving them a free country in which to live.

But we mustn't tarry long, for the time is getting short. Back home, I'd spend some time alone with Vickie. We'd talk about personal things. I'd caution her to be good and to live a Christian life. I'd tell her how proud I am of her and how much I love her. Then I'd just hold her close.

I'd spend some time alone with Valerie, too; and, because she is a baby, we'd play. I'd read her Mother Goose book for the last time, and I'd just love her and hold her, because babies are so sweet.

Perhaps in the afternoon some friends would stop by. Mother and Dad would come, too; and we'd have a quiet, happy time together.

I'd spend the remaining time with Ed. We'd talk about the girls, their future, and the good years we'd had together. There would be no tears or regrets. There'd be no time for that. We'd just be quiet and enjoy the comforting presence of each other. As my last minutes drew to a close, he would kiss me tenderly and tell me that he loved me; and our parting words would be, "Until we meet again." [7]

You might take a biblical personality and write your own interpretation of his life. The personality of the apostle Paul has been a favorite subject for writers, artists, and musicians for centuries. The reason for it is rather obvious. Outside the person of our Lord, the character of Paul has more potential for creative interpretation than perhaps any person in history.

Read below the story of his dramatic conversion on the road to Damascus. As you read the account, put yourself in the position of a dramatist or director who is trying to find a person to play the role of Paul. What will this man have to look like, his facial features? His build? His walk? What temperament and emotional traits must the person have to play the part?

Read a line or two. Then stop and ask, What does this reveal about Paul's personality? When you have read the Scripture passage and made notes, write out a short description of Paul's personality.

> Meanwhile Saul was still breathing murderous threats against the disciples of the Lord. He went to the High Priest and applied for letters to the synagogues at Damascus authorizing him to arrest anyone he found, men or women, who followed the new way, and bring them to Jerusalem. While he was still on the road and nearing Damascus, suddenly a light flashed from the sky all around him. He fell to the ground and heard a voice saying, "Saul, Saul, why do you persecute me?" "Tell me, Lord" he said, "who you are." The voice answered, "I am Jesus, whom you are persecuting. But get up and go into the city, and you will be told what you have to do." Meanwhile the men who were travelling with him stood speechless; they heard the voice but could see no one. Saul got up from the ground, but when he opened his eyes he could not see; so they led him by the hand and brought him into Damascus. He was blind for three days, and took no food or drink (Acts 9:1–9, NEB).

We have attempted in this chapter to give you some clues as to how to stimulate and motivate the learner. These clues are techniques and subtechniques which are derived from motivation research and sensitivity training. The use of these techniques is to be considered as germinal. They are designed to spark interest and create conversation or dialogue.

The suggestions given are just a few of the many possibilities. You can apply the ideas to many different types of adult learning groups. Remember that the techniques should be used with other methods to provide sequence, balance, and comprehensiveness.

6

Evaluating
the Learning
Experience

You will never know whether learning has taken place until you consult the learner. It is doubtful that you will make much progress in your growth as a leader until you are willing to have your leadership performance measured.

Evaluation, then, has two chief concerns. The first concerns testing the outcomes of learning. The second seeks to lift the level of leadership ability. To neglect evaluation of learning is a serious matter. All of us, beginning and mature leaders alike, need to learn how to utilize evaluation techniques.

The thesis of this chapter is that a new degree of efficiency will come to adult learning programs when learning is systematically evaluated.

Reasons for Evaluating Learning

Several reasons for evaluating learning are rather obvious as you begin to explore the subject.

To determine learner growth.—The leader of adults must be

concerned with the total personality of the learner. Jesus stated the ultimate direction of growth for adults when he said, "'Be ye therefore perfect, even as your Father which is in heaven is perfect'" (Matt. 5:48). The leader's guidance of the learner toward this ideal of Christlike character is a responsibility from which he cannot escape.

Each leader should continuously observe each learner for evidences that growth "in favor with God" is taking place. It is possible for you to lead and work with the learner on Sunday and not be aware of the growth or lack of it within the learner.

To discover what learners need.—If a leader knows the life problems and difficulties of the learners, he can direct the activities of learning toward meeting those needs.

One leader was aware that a talented member of the group was embarrassed by an unfortunate circumstance that occurred within her family. As a result, she had withdrawn from the group to avoid conversation with her friends. The leader insisted that she assume responsibility in a learning session. He provided encouragement and resourceful suggestion. The excellent performance by the member was rewarded by the praise of the group. In the experience, the member discovered that her freinds were lovingly concerned about her, and the warmth of their friendship, which she had closed to them, could now be of help to her.

Some needs of members may be so serious as to require the additional help of the pastor or other community helpers. Every leader should be alert to discover the important needs of learners. This knowledge will help determine the goals and activities of learning.

To improve weaknesses in the learning process.—It will amaze you how many little "bugs" will creep into the learning process. The room may be too small and improperly ventilated. The chairs may be uncomfortable. Learners may be facing a bright light. Noise and confusion around the classroom may be bothersome.

You, the leader, may be oblivious to these problems. Periodically, you might give a blank sheet of paper to the members and say; "Write down everything about the setting of learning that bothers you."

Very often, learning is weakened because learners do not understand how to study the material. Some may not have learned how to study in earlier school experiences. The study habits of some adults have been dulled due to inactivity. On occasion, ask learners to answer the following questions:

1. What problems did you encounter in the study of the material?
2. What terminology or words were not carefully defined?
3. How interested were you in the subject?
4. What learning skills were required of you for which you felt inadequate?

The answers to these questions will provide you with a clue as to special study helps the learner may need.

To measure the quality of instruction.—You need a daring, courageous spirit to open yourself up to the constructive criticism of others. But the leader who frequently asks the class, "How am I doing?" is the one who is more likely to mature in his leadership role. Satisfactions should never be such as to make the leader self-satisfied. The anticipatory spirit of the apostle Paul is worthy of emulation. Remember he said, "Not that I have already obtained it, or have already become perfect, but I press on . . . reaching forward to what lies ahead" (Phil. 3:12-13, NASB).*

Frequently, I have asked my students in the seminary classroom to evaluate their teacher's performance during the semester. Their suggestions have been invaluable to my growth as a teacher. At the conclusion of a unit of study, give learners a sheet of blank paper and ask them to answer this question, "How did the leader fail you during the study?"

Sometimes the best kind of evaluation will be your own self-criticism. In *Guiding Adults in Bible Study,* Gaines Dobbins sug-

---

* *New American Standard Bible, New Testament,* © copyright The Lockman Foundation, 1960, 1962, 1963, La Habra, California. Used by permission.

gests that the following questions be periodically asked and answered by the leader:

"Is my enthusiasm for teaching increasing?
Is my concern for each member of the class deepening?
Am I giving enough time to preparation?
Am I gaining more skill in the use of varied methods?
Am I securing participation on the part of all class members?
Is the class showing increasing evidence of Bible study and
   use of what is learned?
Are there observable changes in the lives of members?
Am I myself growing in both knowledge and grace?" [1]

To honestly answer these questions will help you face up to weak points that need strengthening.

READILY OBSERVABLE EVIDENCE OF EFFECTIVE LEARNING

While it is virtually impossible to fully determine the ultimate outcomes of learning, there are some clearly observable signs. W. L. Howse, in *Guiding Young People in Bible Study,* helps us identify some of these.

Group attendance.—Some, these days, take delight in minimizing numerical success. In spite of this fact, increase in attendance and the maintenance of a good average attendance is a solid evidence of effective learning. Avoid the temptation to stimulate attendance artificially. However, continuing faithfulness on the part of members says something about the quality of the learning fellowship. At a Glorieta Training Union Conference, an elderly South Texas dentist remarked, "I don't dare miss our training meeting. There is always something creative and exciting happening which helps me be a better man." His enthusiastic comment revealed a great deal about the kind of learning that takes place in his group.

Learner attention.—The attention of the learner is a real test of effective instruction. No matter how long it takes to achieve it, the attention of the learner must be a major goal of the leader.

The lack of attention will tell you a great deal about the quality of your leadership.

Growth in Christian concepts and character.—Successful learning leadership is always characterized by the changed lives of learners. Christian character is the sum total of what a person is. Effective leadership will assist adults in the development of good habits and the discarding of bad ones.

What a person is will be revealed by what he does. The behavior patterns of learners away from the environment of the church classroom is a good evaluation of your leadership. Is the learner selfish and covetous? Does he live primarily for pleasure? Does he spend his money with little regard for spiritual values? Is the learner utilizing his talents in the service of God? Does the learner waste time? Does his life show evidence of Bible study, prayer, and worship? Does he seek to know and do the will of God? Is his discernment of spiritual things showing evidence of growth? These are the kinds of questions that provide a clue to the spiritual growth of the learner. By seeking answers to these questions, the leader will be evaluating his work.

The Achievement Guide.—Reaching and maintaining various steps of the Achievement Guide is an all-inclusive measurement of your leadership. The Achievement Guide, adopted by your group as a program of work, will create a more favorable climate of learning.

The Achievement Guide is flexible enough to provide direction and recognition for all types of groups in all sizes of churches. Refer to the adult administration books for an explanation of its use.

The continued use of the Achievement Guide will reveal accomplishment and work which remains to be done. Following it as a road map to quality work will keep your group church-centered, keep it from going off on a tangent, and provide a balanced procedure for the work of the group.

The use of the Achievement Guide in adult learning can be a very practical tool of evaluation. Structured evaluation and measurement in education is functionally what inspection is to industry. It enables the organization goal to be more perfectly achieved.

Number of new members reached.—Evidence of successful leadership may be found in the number of new members identifying with your groups. In the Bible teaching program, the teacher should be vitally concerned with the number of unsaved and unenlisted persons who are being attracted to the learning fellowship. The church member training leader should seek to enlist untrained and unenlisted church members in the group he leads. Missionary education leaders should be aggressive in communicating the possibilities of learning to potential members. If a group is reaching out to reach the noninvolved, it is indicative of a leader whose leadership is effective.

HELPING LEARNERS MEASURE LEARNING PROGRESS *

Effective learning in adult groups is dependent upon careful preparation, detailed planning, and skilful execution. Likewise, the learning which results from these groups cannot be guessed at nor judged intuitively.

It is important that the adult learner be able to see progress. If his learning efforts are measurably productive, he is a happy learner. If he leaves the learning experience with new confidence and is able to say, "This I know now, that I didn't know before," his interest and appreciation are heightened.

One of the best ways to help the learner measure his learning progress is with the use of tests. Adult groups in the past, perhaps because of unpleasant associations, were noncongenial with tests. For the most part, this is no longer true. Adults can have a pleasant and rewarding experience with tests without being threatened or embarrassed.

Suitable tests have not always been available in the curriculum materials. This is no longer the case. Writers of content and

---

* Material on pp. 137-144 is adapted from an article by James D. Williams, "Use of a Test," *Young People's Training Guide,* January-March, 1968, pp. 5-7.

teaching or training procedures are building these measurement devices into the materials. It is important, however, that you understand how tests may be constructed and used. There will be times when you will want to prepare your own or modify those which appear in the curriculum.

GUIDING PRINCIPLES IN TEST CONSTRUCTION

Of the many principles that could be cited which would aid in the choice of testing material, two are especially significant. The two guiding principles of any test are its *reliability* and its *validity*.

The reliability of a test, or the accuracy with which it measures something in a particular group, is one aspect of the validity of the test. The concept of validity, on the other hand, refers to the extent to which the test serves its purpose with the group for which it was intended.

TESTING FORMS WHICH LEADERS MAY USE

1. *Essay.*—These tests theoretically are given in order that a learner may gather his thoughts from a well-stocked memory, sift them out, and apply them to the topic at hand.

This type of test is usually introduced with a word such as *discuss, describe, explain,* or *compare.* However, there are some weaknesses with this type of questioning which makes its validity and reliability of less value than other kinds of tests. Some of these weaknesses are:

(1) It is easy to pad answers, rather than answering with specific material.

(2) The discussion may go contrary to the concept of the constructor of the test.

(3) Often there is a lack of logic in this type of test.

(4) The test actually measures only a sample of the knowledge because of the scope of the test.

2. *Objective.*—The short-answer objective test is based upon two principles: *simple recall* and *completion* or recognition. This type of test is perhaps the simplest to use. The types of objective tests are many. The following are examples:

(1) Simple-recall.—One of the oldest methods of attempting to objectify the response to a test is that of simple recall. Test items may be expressed a. in the form of a question, b. in the form of a statement, or c. in the form of a stimulus word.

(2) Sentence-completion.—This test should possess three characteristics: a. the blanks in the sentence should all be the same length, b. all of the blanks should be numbered, and c. the correspondingly numbered blanks should be placed in a vertical column to the right or left of the sentences.

(3) Multiple-choice.—In this type of short-answer test the right answer appears among a number of wrong ones (usually two to four). Unless the wrong answers are as plausible as the right ones, the test has little validity or reliability.

(4) Alternative response (may include true-false, yes-no, agree-disagree, right-wrong).—The criteria of this test is a judgment rendered as to whether a statement is right or wrong.

(5) Matching.—Two parts are necessary: a. a list of sentences in each of which an esential word or phrase is omitted, and b. a list of words which contains the best answer for each omitted word or phrase.

(6) Evaluation.—The purpose of evaluation is to discover areas of weaknesses and to discover means of improving them. The test is based on a rating scale which is the basis for evaluation.

3. *Interest*.—There are several methods which may be used in discovering interest.

(1) The direct method.—This method involves going directly to the subject and asking him about his interest. Simple questions will probably suffice to give you the information you desire.

(2) The observation method.—This method involves the observation of various criteria. Noticing the presence of well-worn children's books on a bookrack together with others which are clean and new is an example of this type of observation.

(3) The assumption method.—This method involves the assumption that the greater amount of information a person possesses in a certain area, the greater will be his interest in that area.

4. *Attitude.*—There are five characteristics of attitudes which must be known before accurate testing may take place.

(1) An attitude is essentially a set feeling or disposition.

(2) An attitude involves a feeling to act favorably or unfavorably, positively or negatively toward an object.

(3) An attitude is the result of an experience.

(4) An attitude is directed toward some object, such as a person, a race, an institution, or an idea.

(5) An attitude is difficult to change.

In measuring an attitude, Jordan says,

> The ideal situation would be to have a series of unambiguous statements placed at equal intervals on a scale ranging from absolute approval to absolute disapproval. Each statement would be chosen because it expressed clearly and certainly a defined position on the scale. A person wishing to discover his own attitude could then check the items or statements with which he agreed, add up the positional points and divide this sum by their number, thus obtaining his position on the scale.[2]

5. *Personality.*—Personality inventories and tests possess some traits and characteristics not included in tests of intelligence or of achievement. More particularly, these inventories refer to aspects of emotional adjustment which contribute to personality balance and integration. These tests are usually objective in their approach, but the fundamental end is an evaluation related to the individual's personality.

ILLUSTRATIONS OF TESTING FORMS

The following will represent hypothetical illustrations of the various types of tests discussed.

1. Essay.—The lesson concerns the urgency of our task as Christians. Scripture references: John 4:25-38; Acts 4:18-20. The following are possible essay questions:

(1) Describe what obstacles you face most frequently when you are trying to win someone to Christ.

(2) Based on the above Scripture passages, explain what procedures you would use to speed the outreach of your church.

2. Objective

(1) SIMPLE-RECALL

    a. Question: In the Great Commission, what was the imperative command which followed the command to "go"? ____

_____

    b. Statement: Give the number of men who stood by after the ascension of Christ. _____

    c. Stimulus-word: Mount of Olives _____

_____

(2) SENTENCE-COMPLETION: Jesus commanded his disciples to (a) ____ into all nations and to (b) ____ as well as (c) ____ them. Christ promised at the close of his statement that he would be with us until the end of ____ (d) ____.

(3) MULTIPLE-CHOICE: Scripture reference: John 4:25-38.

    a. The Samaritan woman, because her life was sinful, was (a) embarrassed, (b) reluctant, (c) eager, (d) unashamed to talk to the Master.

    b. The Samaritan woman was considered an unlikely prospect for salvation because of her (a) sex, (b) profession, (c) race, (d) loose character.

(4) ALTERNATIVE RESPONSES (true-false; yes-no; agree-disagree; right-wrong):

    a. True-False: If we follow Jesus' example, seeking the lost would have priority in our lives.

    b. Yes-No: Jesus was polite to the woman at the well but never really appreciated her presence.

    c. Agree-Disagree: Jesus should never have spoken to the woman because of the racial barrier.

d. Right-Wrong: The woman felt her temple of worship was just as important as the Temple at Jerusalem.

(5) MATCHING: Scripture reference: Romans 9:1-10:13.

A. ( ) gospel
B. ( ) Romans
C. ( ) grace
D. ( ) condemnation
E. ( ) redemption
(a) Pauline epistle
(b) doomed to death
(c) pardon from sin
(d) good news
(e) unmerited favor

(6) EVALUATION: Topic, "Bible Study Habits"

a. I have a quiet time every morning with God. 0 1 2 3 4 5

b. Was the Scripture reading for today pertinent to daily living? 0 1 2 3 4 5

c. Is my quiet time mechanical? 0 1 2 3 4 5

d. Was there evidence of a sense of purpose and direction in my Bible study? 0 1 2 3 4 5

3. Interest.—(These tests are primarily concerned with finding areas of interest for further study or can be used as carryover tools to build interest in the next session.)

(1) FINDING AREAS OF INTEREST FOR FURTHER STUDY

a. Which of the epistles have you enjoyed most?

(a) _____
(b) _____
(c) _____

b. Which epistle would you like to concentrate on in a comprehensive study?

(a) _____
(b) _____
(c) _____

c. Of the New Testament writers, which three are your favorites?

(a) _____

(b) _____

(c) _____

    d. Which of the following would you rather do? (a) Study the New Testament, (b) study the Old Testament (c) study individual books.

    (2) SECURING MEANINGFUL CARRYOVER

    a. Of the following subjects, which one interests you the most? *Sanctification, justification, grace.*

    b. What interests you most about Paul's letter to Rome? (a) All have sinned, (b) all can be saved, (c) man is hopelessly lost.

    c. What do you consider the most important point emphasized in the letter to the Romans? (a) The depravity of man, (b) the relationship of Christ to his church, (c) a salvation for all.

4. *Attitude*

    (1) ATTITUDES TOWARD THE NEGRO: Place a plus (+) mark if you agree with the statement. Place a minus (−) if you disagree.

    ☐ *a.* The differences between the black and white races are not of degree but of kind.

    ☐ *b.* No Negro should hold an office of trust and honor.

    ☐ *c.* The Negro and the white are inherently equal.

    ☐ *d.* The Negro is by no means fit for social equality with the white man.

    (2) COMPANIONS SELECTED FOR A VARIETY OF SITUATIONS (a test of attitudes in a study of prejudice): The pictures are numbered 1-12. The attitude test involves the numbers and pictures.

    a. Show me all those that you want to sit next to you on a bus. (Numbered pictures show Negro and white children.)

    b. Show me all you would like to have as members of your church.

c. Show me those you would like to recommend for your job when you are promoted.

d. Show me those you would like to live next door to you.

e. Show me all those you like.

5. *Personality*

(1) CHRISTIAN TRAITS

a. Yes-No: Does it make you uncomfortable to be "different" or "unconventional"?

b. Yes-No: Do you usually work things out for yourself rather than get someone to help you?

c. Yes-No: Have you ever crossed a street to avoid a person?

d. Yes-No: Do you daydream on occasion?

e. Yes-No: Can you stand criticism without being hurt?

(2) HONESTY TRAIT TEST. Select one answer in each situation.

a. Philip dropped and broke his mother's favorite phonograph record. He knew his mother would feel bad about it. _____ *He should tell his mother what happened.* _____ *He should hide the record and not say anything about it.*

b. Henry received a speeding ticket on the way home from the office. He knew Mary would be angry with him. _____ *He should not tell Mary and just pay the fine.* _____ *He should tell Mary because he is honest with her in all things.*

Tests can be fun, can provide excitement and interest, and can enable the learner to learn! In addition, the wise leader can, from tests, measure the effectiveness of his teaching.

An interesting assignment for you would be to study the current materials being used in one of the program organizations of the church. Based on the content of this chapter, prepare a sample test which could be given to learners.

In addition, search the materials to find tests included in the materials. Evaluate these tests in light of the guidelines contained in this chapter. Classify the tests according to their purposes.

Leader and Learners Evaluating the Group Learning Process

Throughout the entire history of the space program, evaluation of systems, equipment, and training procedures has been integral to the development of the program. Learning, likewise, will never get off the ground unless it too comes under the judicious scrutiny of learners and leader.

Some new tools of evaluation.—Developments in the field of electronics have made possible some exciting tools of evaluation for group learning. For example, the tape recorder is now within the financial reach of most church groups. Taping a group session and replaying it in the presence of the group will help the group discipline itself to its own learning needs. Overly talkative members are made aware of their loquaciousness. Poorly prepared participants discover the negative influence their lack of preparation made. Verbal mannerisms of the leader and learners are revealed. Listening to a replay of the group session allows for review and reinforcement of the learning content.

Some churches are now buying video tape machines. These are being used in a variety of ways in the church's educational program. Can you visualize how effective it would be for an adult group to be able to see and hear itself in "learning action"?

Standard tools of evaluation.—There are other educationally valid evaluation instruments which the group may use. One noted educator has pointed out that the best kind of evaluation is the subjective, spontaneous, written opinion of the learner. All you need to do is give him a blank sheet of paper and ask him three simple questions: What did you like best? What did you like least? What was most helpful to you?

A little more sophisticated evaluation form can be reproduced and used for postreaction. The following types of questions can be used or modified. A word of caution: don't ask the learner to answer too many questions. He may be overwhelmed and "hush up," causing you to miss some of his best insights.

1. *General questions**

(1) What did you like best about the session (or unit)? Least? What was most helpful to you?

(2) What did you learn from the session (or unit)?

(3) What specific things came up that you would have liked to explore further?

(4) How would you suggest the session (unit study) could have been improved?

(5) Very honestly, what is your impression of the session (unit study)?

(6) Do you honestly feel that members in your group really care about each other?

(7) What would you say is the greatest need in your spiritual life at this moment?

(8) Do you feel "safe" in discussing the deepest needs of your life with those in your group?

2. *Contrasting questions* [3]

(1) How did you like the session today?

Excellent 5 4 3 2 1 Poor

(2) Were the purposes clear?

Very clear 5 4 3 2 1 Not clear

(3) How well did the group work together?

Very well 5 4 3 2 1 Poorly

(4) How did you feel as a member of the group?

Accepted 5 4 3 2 1 Rejected

(5) How did you feel that the subject matter was presented?   Very well 5 4 3 2 1 Poorly

(6) How did you feel about participating in the discussion?   Very free 5 4 3 2 1 Very inhibited

(7) How interested were you in the topic?

Very interested 5 4 3 2 1 Not at all interested

(8) Did you gain any new ideas or insights about the problem?   Many 5 4 3 2 1 None

---

* Adapted from *40 Ways to Teach in Groups* by Martha M. Leypoldt. (See Bibliography.)

(9) How suitable was the method of teaching?

Very suitable 5 4 3 2 1 Not at all suitable

(10) How relaxed did you feel?

Completely relaxed 5 4 3 2 1 Extremely tense

INSTRUMENT FOR TESTING YOUR BIBLE TEACHING

It would be a helpful and wholesome exercise to grade yourself as a teacher, using the following marks: for each question on which you would grade yourself *excellent*, mark 5, for those *good*, mark 3, and for those *fair*, mark 0. If total amounts to 80 or above, you would rank as an excellent teacher, 60 to 80, a good teacher, and under 60, a fair teacher. Grade yourself each quarter and then compare your grades.

PREPARATION

— Do you look through the lesson topics in advance?

— Do you begin lesson preparation in advance of more than a week?

— Is the Bible itself the center of your lesson preparation?

— Do you have a systematic plan of lesson study?

— Do you keep definite needs of all of your pupils in mind as you prepare?

— Do you seek constantly to improve your teaching by general reading, by attending teachers' meetings, training courses?

— Do you pray much about your task?

PRESENTATION

— Are you able to stimulate interest from the very beginning?

— Do your pupils use their Bibles during the lesson period?

— Do your pupils—all of them—participate in the lesson discussion?

— Do you use a variety of teaching methods?

— Do you follow the main subject to a desirable goal or do you sidetrack?

— Do you schedule your presentation to give proper emphasis to the central theme or truth?

— Do you and your pupils reach definite and practical conclusions at the end of each lesson period?

EVALUATION

— Does your teaching stimulate your pupils to more Bible study?

— Does your teaching change pupils' moral and social standards of living?

— Does your teaching win the lost to Christ?

— Does your teaching make pupils more faithful in their church relationships?

— Does your teaching make *you* a better Christian?

—— Total score

An ancient proverb says, "A man who has committed a mistake and doesn't correct it is committing another mistake." If the learner has learned something wrong or has failed to learn, this error needs correcting. One of the most important tasks of the leader is to help learners be aware of their shortcomings. Analysis and experience with fact-finding, checking, and proving will lift the level of learning.

It is likewise a mistake to discover errors or weaknesses in one's leadership performance and then fail to do anything about them. You must *decide* to improve, and then *act*. Some leaders get excited about using new approaches, but never do anything about it. They may be compared to an oven that is always heating up but seldom baking anything. Be critical enough to discover leadership errors and then judicious enough to do something about them.

Near the close of his public ministry, Jesus prayed, "For their sakes I sanctify myself" (John 17:19). Should this not be the desire and goal of all Christian leaders? For the sake of learners whom we seek to lead and for the sake of Christ whom we seek to serve, we dare not do less.

Personal Learning Activities

Chapter 1

1. Why is Christian Adult education a new imperative for our time?
2. Why is it necessary for Adults to continue in learning?
3. How would you define *learning*?
4. What is the relationship between learning and character?
5. List eight characteristics of Adult learning.
6. What particular characteristics have you observed in the Adult group of which you are a member?

Chapter 2

1. What are some misconceptions concerning the role of a learning leader?
2. How would you define *teaching*?
3. Reconstruct your own model of the teaching process using the model given in this chapter.
4. Identify the three different types of learning outcomes a leader may desire for learners.
5. Identify the major steps in a good teaching plan.
6. What personal qualities do you need to develop in order to strengthen your leadership skills?

Chapter 3

1. In your own words, state what is meant by *learning goal*.
2. Identify six factors which the leader must consider when writing a learning goal.
3. What word describes the first or basic level of learning? What word or words describe the deepest level of learning?
4. Suppose you had the responsibility of teaching the content of this chapter to a group of Adults. Write out a learning goal or goals you would use in that assignment.

Chapter 4

1. How would you define *teaching method?*
2. How do learning outcomes affect the choice of methods?
3. What is an argument for keeping Adult learning groups in the church relatively small?
4. Of the methods discussed in this chapter, list those which you have never used or observed before.
5. Select a learning goal (perhaps the one you wrote in the questions for chapter 3) and choose the methods you would use in the learning session that would be based on that method.

Chapter 5

1. What is meant by *motivation?*
2. Is motivation primarily an internal or external process?
3. Give examples of internal and external motivation.
4. Briefly describe some ways you as a leader might use to attract Adults to the learning situation.
5. Name several techniques a leader can use to help hold the learners attention during a learning experience.
6. Construct your own example of the following techniques and explain how they could be used in a teaching situation: (1) completion technique, (2) word association tests, (3) choice of ordering techniques, (4) an expressive technique.

Chapter 6

1. Briefly identify the two chief concerns of instructional evaluation.
2. List and briefly explain the major reasons for evaluating learning.
3. What are some readily observable evidences of effective learning?
4. What are the two major types of tests?
5. Read last Sunday's Sunday School lesson and prepare an objective test based on its content.
6. In your own words write a brief paragraph on the subject, "How to Evaluate the Learning Process."

The New Church Study Course

THE New Church Study Course, effective in January 1970 is based on more than three years of study and design. It offers several improvements in the Church Study Course, which began in October, 1959. At that time three courses previously promoted by the Sunday School Board were merged: the Sunday School Training Course, the Graded Training Union Study Course, and the Church Music Training Course. Principles and methods books of the Woman's Missionary Union and the Brotherhood Commission were added in October 1961 and January 1967 respectively.

The New Church Study Course offers increased flexibility in meeting the needs of Southern Baptists. It provides courses of varying length and difficulty, varied formats and types of course materials, additional types of credit, and improved organization of courses.

The New Church Study Course consists of two types of courses: the Christian Development Courses for all church members and the Christian Leadership Courses for church leaders. These courses are organized into subject areas.

The purpose of Christian Development Courses is to provide courses of study which will help church members grow toward maturity in Christian living and competence in Christian service. These courses offer more comprehensive, advanced, and varied learning experiences in subject areas of a church's educational program than can be provided through curriculum periodicals. Tests and exercises, credits, and diplomas of achievement which help church members measure their progress in developing needed knowledge, understanding, and skills are included in some courses. Units of instruction are provided for Preschoolers and Children. These are designed to reinforce foundational learnings. Materials which churches may use in recognizing the participation of Children in these units are available from Baptist Book Stores.

Christian Leadership Courses provide a comprehensive series of courses organized into subject areas dealing with knowledge, understandings, and skills needed for effective church leadership. Tests and exercises and credits and diplomas to help leaders measure their growth in leadership ability are included in some courses. The Christian Leadership Courses are the primary source for leadership training materials prepared by the agencies cooperating in the New Church Study Course.

Courses in both series are designed to be effective for individual and class study. Learning aids, study guides, and teaching guides are available for some courses. Credits are granted to Youth and Adults for reading, individual study, and class study.

The New Church Study Course is promoted by the Sunday School Board, 127 Ninth Avenue, North, Nashville, Tennessee 37203, through the departments in the Education Division; by the Woman's Missionary Union, 600 Morth Twentieth Street, Birmingham, Alabama 35203; by the Brotherhood Commission, 1548 Poplar Avenue, Memphis, Tennessee 38104; and by the respective departments in the state conventions affiliated with the Southern Baptist Convention.

A record of all credits and diplomas earned should be maintained in each church.

Detailed information about the course and the system of credits, diplomas, and record keeping is available from the agencies listed above.

Forms for keeping records may be ordered from any Baptist Book Store.

Requirements for Credit

THIS BOOK is the text for course 6110 of subject area 1 of Christian Leadership Courses, New Church Study Course. If credit is desired for this course through class study, individual study, or reading, the following requirements must be met:

I. Classwork

1. This course is designed for seven and one half (7½) hours of class study and carries three (3) credits for such usage. If the course is studied in a class setting of less than seven and one half (7½) hours, the following criteria apply:

    (1) Five (5) class hours—two (2) credits

    (2) Two and one half (2½) class hours—one (1) credit

    The teacher will indicate the length of the class and the number of credits to be granted on Form 151, Request for Course Credit (revised). For courses in which laboratory experience or practice is desirable, two (2) hours of such guided experience may be substituted as one (1) hour of class time, provided at least half of the required hours are actually spent in classwork.

2. A class member who attends all class sessions and completes the reading of the book as directed by the teacher will not be required to do any written work for credit.

3. A class member who is absent from one or more sessions must complete the required exercises or questions in the "Personal Learning Activities" section on all chapters he misses. In such a case, he must turn in his paper by the date the teacher sets (usually within ten days following the last class). Also, he must certify that he has read the book.

4. The teacher should request credits for himself. A person who teaches a course for Youth or Adults (in any subject area) will be granted the same number of credits as class members. The teacher of an approved unit of study of Preschoolers and

Children will be granted two credits in course 6299 in subject area 62 of Christian Leadership Courses. Request credits on Form 151.

5. The church training director or the person designated by the church should complete Form 151, Request for Course Credit (revised), and forward it after completion of the class to the Church Study Course Awards Office, 127 Ninth Avenue, North, Nashville, Tennessee 37203.

II. Individual Study

1. A person who wishes to complete this course without attending class sessions may receive full credit by certifying that he has read the book and has completed all exercises or questions in the "Personal Learning Activities" section.

2. Students may find profit in studying the text together, but individual papers are required. Carbon copies or duplicates of the answers cannot be accepted.

3. The work required for individual study credit should be turned in for checking to the church training director or the person designated by the church to administer The New Church Study Course. Form 151, Request for Course Credit (revised), must be used in requesting credits. It is to be forwarded by the church training director or the person designated by the church to the Church Study Course Awards Office, 127 Ninth Avenue, North, Nashville, Tennessee 37203.

III. Reading Credit

1. A person may receive one (1) credit toward the diploma on which he is working by reading this book.

2. Upon completion of the reading, he must complete Form 151, Request for Course Credit (revised). He should give the completed form to the church training director or to the person designated by his church to be responsible for administering The New Church Study Course.

3. The church training director or the person designated by the church will see that the request is completed, signed, and forwarded to the Church Study Course Awards Office, 127 Ninth Avenue, North, Nashville, Tennessee 37203.

IV. Awards and Records

Two copies of the course credit award form will be sent by the Church Study Course Awards Office to the church. The original copy should be filed in the church training record and the duplicate given to the individual.

Notes

Chapter 1

1. Charles R. Stinnette, *Learning in Theological Perspective* (New York: Association Press, 1965), p. 68. Used by permission.
2. Robert S. Clemmons, *Education for Churchmanship* (Nashville: Abingdon Press, 1966), p. 82. Used by permission.
3. Paul Bergevin, *A Philosophy for Adult Education* (New York: The Seabury Press, 1967), p. 121. Used by permission.
4. *Ibid.*, pp. 122-123.

Chapter 2

1. John T. Sisemore, *Blueprint for Teaching* (Nashville: Broadman Press, 1964), p. 52. Used by permission.
2. Findley B. Edge, *Teaching for Results* (Nashville: Broadman Press, 1956), p. 97. Used by permission.
3. Sisemore, *op. cit.*, p. 58.
4. Adapted from Edge, *op. cit.*, pp. 81-83.

Chapter 4

1. Sara Little, *Learning Together in the Christian Fellowship* (Richmond: John Knox Press, 1956), p. 22. Used by permission.
2. Adapted from Martha M. Leypoldt, *40 Ways to Teach in Groups* (Valley Forge: The Judson Press, 1967), pp. 44-45.

Chapter 5

1. Mehran K. Thomson, "Motivation in School Learning," Charles E. Skinner, Editor, *Educational Psychology, Fourth Edition,* © 1959, p. 450. Reprinted by permission of Prentice-Hall, Inc., Englewood Cliffs, New Jersey.
2. John McKinley, *Creative Methods for Adult Classes* (St. Louis: The Bethany Press, 1960), p. 29. Used by permission.
3. Harry L. Miller, *Teaching and Learning in Adult Education* (New York: The Macmillan Company, 1964), p. 39. Used by permission.
4. William H. Burton, *The Guidance of Learning Activities* (New York: Appleton-Century-Crofts, Educational Division, Meredith Corporation, 1952), p. 69. Used by permission.
5. Skinner, *op. cit.*, p. 456.
6. McKinley, *op. cit.*, p. 18.
7. From *The Baptist Training Union Magazine,* November, 1968, p. 40.

156

Chapter 6

1. Gaines S. Dobbins, *Guiding Adults in Bible Study* (Nashville: Convention Press, 1960), p. 127.
2. A. M. Jordan, *Measurement in Education* (New York: McGraw-Hill Book Co., Inc., 1953), p. 41. Used with permission of McGraw-Hill Book Company.
3. Adapted from Leypoldt, *op. cit.*, p. 119.

Bibliography

Bell, Shirley. "If I Had Twenty-four Hours to Live," *The Baptist Training Union Magazine*. Vol. 43, No. 11 (November, 1968).

Bergevin, Paul. *A Philosophy for Adult Education*. New York: The Seabury Press, 1967.

Bergevin, Paul, *et al. Adult Education Procedures, A Handbook of Tested Patterns for Effective Participation*. New York: The Seabury Press, 1963.

Bergevin, Paul and Dwight Morris. *Group Processes for Adult Education*. New York: The Seabury Press, 1955.

Bertolet, Dorothy. *Ways of Teaching*. Philadelphia: The Westminster Press, 1965.

Bittel, L. R. and R. L. Craig. *Training and Development Handbook*. New York: McGraw-Hill Book Company, 1967.

Bloom, B. S., *et al. Taxonomy of Educational Objectives; Handbook I: Cognitive Domain and Taxonomy of Educational Objectives*, 1956; *Handbook II: Affective Domain*, 1964. New York: McKay Company.

Bonhoeffer, Dietrich. *The Cost of Discipleship*. New York: The Macmillan Company, 1949.

Bowman, Jr., Locke E. J. *Straight Talk About Teaching in Today's Church*. Philadelphia: The Westminster Press, 1967.

Burton, William H. *The Guidance of Learning Activities*. New York: Appleton-Century-Crofts, Inc., 1944.

Clemmons, Robert S. *Education for Churchmanship*. Nashville: Abingdon Press, 1966.

Clevenger, Theodore. *Audience Analysis*. Indianapolis: The Bobbs-Merrill Company, Inc., 1966.

Coleman, John E. *The Master Teachers and the Art of Teaching*. New York: Pitman Publishing Company.

Coleman, Lucien, Jr. *Understanding Adults*. Nashville: Convention Press, 1969.

Coleman, Lyman. *Acts Alive*. New York: Oxford University Press, 1961.

———. *Coffee House Itch*. New York: Oxford University Press, 1961.

Colson, Howard P. *Preparing to Teach the Bible*. Nashville: Convention Press, 1959.

Cram, David. *Explaining Teaching Machines and Programming*. San Francisco: Fearon Publishers, 1961.

Crow, Lester D. and Alice. *Human Development and Learning*. New York: American Book Company, 1956.

DeCecco, John P. *Educational Technology: Readings in Programmed Instruction.* New York: Harper & Row, Publishers, 1966.

Dichter, Ernest. *The Strategy of Desire.* New York: Doubleday and Company, Inc., 1960.

Dobbins, Gaines S. *Guiding Adults in Bible Study.* Nashville: Convention Press, 1960.

Downie, N. M. *Fundamentals of Measurement, Principals and Practices.* New York: Oxford University Press, 1967.

Drakeford, John. *The Awesome Power of the Listening Ear.* Waco: Word Publishers, Inc. 1967.

Edge, Findley B. *Helping the Teacher.* Nashville: Broadman Press, 1959.

———. *Quest for Vitality in Religion.* Nashville: Broadman Press, 1963.

———. *Teaching for Results.* Nashville: Broadman Press, 1956.

Ernsberger, David J. *A Philosophy of Adult Christian Education.* Philadelphia: The Westminster Press, 1959.

Ford, LeRoy. *A Primer for Teachers and Leaders.* Nashville: Broadman Press, 1963.

———. *Tools for Teaching and Training.* Nashville: Broadman Press, 1963.

———. *Using the Case Study in Teaching and Training.* Nashville: Broadman Press, 1970.

———. *Using the Lecture in Teaching and Training.* Nashville: Broadman Press, 1968.

Fry, John R. *A Hard Look at Adult Christian Education.* Philadelphia: The Westminster Press, 1961.

Glen, J. Stanley. *The Recovery of the Teaching Ministry.* Philadelphia: The Westminster Press, 1967.

Hare, Paul A., *et al. Small Groups, Studies in Social Interaction.* New York: Alfred A. Knopf, 1955.

Henry, Harry. *Motivation Research.* New York: Ungar, Frederick Publishing Company, 1958.

Hurlock, Elizabeth A. *Developmental Psychology.* New York: McGraw-Hill Book Company, Inc., 1968.

Ishee, John A. *Adults in Church Training.* Nashville: Broadman Press, 1969.

Jordan, A. M. *Measurement in Education.* Out of print.

Klausmeier, H. J. and Goodwin W. *Learning and Human Abilities: Educational Psychology.* New York: Harper & Row, Publishers, 1966.

Klein, Alan F. *Role Playing in Leadership Training and Group Problem Solving.* New York: Association Press, 1956.

Leypoldt, Martha M. *40 Ways to Teach in Groups.* Valley Forge: The Judson Press, 1967.

Little, Sara. *Learning Together in the Christian Fellowship.* Richmond: John Knox Press, 1956.

Loessner, Ernest J. *Adults Continuing to Learn.* Nashville: Convention Press, 1967.

Luck, David J., *et al. Marketing Research.* New Jersey: Prentice-Hall, 1961.

Mager, Robert F. *Preparing Objectives for Programmed Instruction*. San Francisco: Fearon Publishers, 1962.

McKinley, John. *Creative Methods for Adult Classes*. St. Louis: The Bethany Press, 1960.

Miller, Harry L. *Teaching and Learning in Adult Education*. New York: The Macmillan Company, 1964.

Murphy, Dennis. *Better Business Communication*. New York: McGraw-Hill Book Company, Inc., 1957.

Pierce, Rice A. *Leading Dynamic Bible Study*. Nashville: Broadman Press, 1969.

Pinson, William, Jr. *How to Deal with Controversial Issues*. Nashville: Broadman Press, 1966.

Price, John Milburn. *Jesus the Teacher*. Nashville: Convention Press, 1960.

Ruesch, Jurgen and Weldon Kees. *NonVerbal Communication*. Out of print.

Salisbury, Hugh M. and Larry Peabody. *A Guide to Effective Bible Teaching*. Grand Rapids: Baker Book House, 1966.

Sisemore, John T. *Blueprint for Teaching*. Nashville: Broadman Press, 1964.

Skinner, Charles E. (ed.) *Educational Psychology, Fourth Edition*. Englewood Cliffs: Prentice-Hall, Inc., 1959.

Smith, Henry Clay. *Sensitivity to People*. New York: McGraw-Hill Book Company, Inc., 1966.

Stinnette, Charles R. *Learning in Theological Perspective*. New York: Association Press, 1965.

Trecker, H. B. and Audrey. *How to Work with Church Groups*. New York: Association Press, 1952.

Wellington, C. B. and Jean. *Teaching for Critical Thinking*. New York: McGraw-Hill Book Company, Inc., 1960.

Zelko, Harold P. *Successful Conference and Discussion Techniques*. New York: McGraw-Hill Book Company, Inc., 1957.

Basic Resources for
Your
Church's Education Program

GUIDING ADULTS gives attention to working with Adults in all the organizations of a church. On the following pages, descriptive of basic resources for each church organization are given.

Sunday School

Adult Sunday School Work is designed for all those who work with adults in Sunday School, with department and class leaders. The book sets forth the challenge of Sunday School work with adults in the 70's. It also provides practical help in organizing and administering adult departments and classes. Special emphasis is given to adding new vitality and enlarged dimensions to adult Sunday School work.

Church Training

Adults in Church Training is a "how to do it" manual on organizing and administering Church Training for Adults. Attention is given to patterns and plans of organization, series of curriculum material, and the dynamics of group work. This volume with its accompanying booklets for leaders projects a comprehensive training program for Adults.

Successful Enlistment is directed toward the enlistment leader. Included in this booklet are appeals and techniques to be used in enlisting Adults in church training.

Creative Group Work is for the training group leader and deals with group dynamics and how to administer the work of a training group.

Efficient Administration is directed toward the department director and deals with the functions related to directing a department in the Adult Church Training Program.

Meaningful Training is directed to the study leader and deals with how to plan, conduct, and evaluate a unit of study.

Music Ministry

Church Music for Adults represents the culmination of four years of study and research. It presents and explains the philosophy, concepts, and organizational patterns of the Adult Division of the Church Music program.

This book is designed for use by those who assume positions of leadership of adults in performing groups and music study groups. If you have such a responsibility, this book is a source of help you can't afford to miss.

The ten chapters of the book deal with the following areas:

1. Why Is an Adult

This chapter is concerned with the adult as a person, and with appropriate ways to motivate adults.

2. The Work to Be Done

The four major tasks of the Church Music program are discussed.

(1) Teach music
(2) Train persons to lead, sing, and play music
(3) Provide music in the church and community
(4) Provide and interpret information regarding the work of the church and the denomination

3. Workers Together

This chapter deals with inter-program relationships.

4. Organization
5. Leaders
6. Members
7. Resources

This discussion deals with both physical and financial resources.

8. Planning
9. Administrative Controls
10. Summary

The importance of this first study course book on adult music work cannot be minimized. The program it reveals and the challenge it affords will inspire music leaders in every Southern Baptist church.

Baptist Men

Baptist Men in Missions is a methods book on how to start and operate a Baptist Men's unit of Brotherhood in a church. Outlines organization, resources, relationships, facilities and administrative controls.

Woman's Missionary Society

Baptist Women Leader Manual
Baptist Women Member Handbook
Baptist Young Women Leader Manual
Baptist Young Women Member Handbook

These resources provide guidance in how to administer an effective program for Baptist women.

Notes

Notes